Warfare in Neolithic Europe

Warfare in Neolithic Europe

An Archaeological and Anthropological Analysis

Julian Heath

PEN & SWORD
ARCHAEOLOGY

First published in Great Britain in 2017 by
Pen & Sword Archaeology
an imprint of
Pen & Sword Books Ltd
47 Church Street
Barnsley
South Yorkshire
S70 2AS

ISBN 978 1 47387 985 0

A CIP catalogue record for this book is
available from the British Library.

Printed and bound in Malta
By Gutenberg Press Ltd.

Pen & Sword Books Ltd incorporates the Imprints of Pen & Sword Books Archaeology, Atlas, Aviation, Battleground, Discovery, Family History, History, Maritime, Military, Naval, Politics, Railways, Select, Transport, True Crime, Fiction, Frontline Books, Leo Cooper, Praetorian Press, Seaforth Publishing, Wharncliffe and White Owl.

For a complete list of Pen & Sword titles please contact
PEN & SWORD BOOKS LIMITED
47 Church Street, Barnsley, South Yorkshire, S70 2AS, England
E-mail: enquiries@pen-and-sword.co.uk
Website: www.pen-and-sword.co.uk

For Pam, with Love

Contents

Acknowledgements

I would like to express my gratitude to all of the individuals who kindly provided images for use in this book, and all of the team at Pen and Sword Books who helped in its preparation and publication.

Introduction

In the Neolithic Age savage warfare did I wage
For food and woolly horses' pelt.
I was singer to my clan in that dim, red Dawn of Man,
And I sang of all we fought and feared and felt.
(Excerpt from *In the Neolithic Age* by Rudyard Kipling, 1895)

The emergence of the Neolithic or 'New Stone Age' undoubtedly represents a pivotal point in human history. During this time, people turned away from a deeply ancient, semi-nomadic lifestyle based on the hunting and gathering of wild animals and plants, to a new one centred on domesticated crops and animals and permanent farming villages (although there is growing evidence that at least some hunter-gatherer communities lived in permanent settlements). This switch from hunting and gathering (or 'foraging' as some archaeologists refer to it) to farming, led the renowned Australian archaeologist Vere Gordon Childe to propose one of the most famous concepts of prehistoric archaeology – the 'Neolithic Revolution'. Although Childe's 'Revolution' is now outdated and somewhat flawed, its underlying premise still holds true, as the emergence of farming in the Neolithic ultimately laid the foundations for the incredibly sophisticated (and socially stratified) modern societies in which many of us live today.

The first farming communities emerged in the Levant c. 9000 BC, although it is now realised that the origins of the Neolithic lie much further back in Near Eastern prehistory. Some 2000 years later, around 7000 BC, the first farmers in mainland Europe were arriving in Greece from western Anatolia, and perhaps also from the Levant. Archaeological evidence found on Cyprus at the sites of Kilmonas and Ayia Varvara-Asprokremnos strongly suggests that PPN (pre-pottery Neolithic) migrants from the Levant made landfall on the island as early as c. 8600 BC. This Cypriot evidence perhaps indicates that the earliest Neolithic sites on Greece may date back to well before the early seventh millennium BC, although as yet, none have come to light. From Greece and the Balkans, the Neolithic then basically spread across the rest of

Europe through a combination of further migration by early farming groups and the adoption of this new lifestyle by indigenous Late Mesolithic communities; finally reaching the shores of Britain and Ireland around 4300–4000 BC. There were two main routes along which this Neolithic lifestyle spread into Europe from Greece and the Balkans: one running along the 'Danubian corridor', and the other along the coastlines of the northern Mediterranean.

From the perspective of our own troubled times, we could be forgiven for looking back through the millennia and seeing the Neolithic as a time when people lived simple and peaceful lives in pristine rural landscapes. However, we would be looking through glasses of a decidedly rosy hue, as archaeologists have discovered – and continue to discover – strong evidence for the existence of warfare amongst many of Europe's first farming communities. This evidence should certainly not be taken as proof that warfare was endemic across Europe during the Neolithic, but it certainly reveals that many more people than we might like to think lost their lives in armed conflicts during this time. Indeed, as we shall see, the words of the seventeenth-century English philosopher, Thomas Hobbes, who famously described prehistoric life as 'nasty, brutish, and short' in his famous work, *Leviathan*,[1] seem rather apt in light of some of the archaeological discoveries from the European Neolithic. Although some still cling to the view that the European Neolithic was essentially peaceful (with a few minor but inconsequential violent skirmishes here and there) the archaeological evidence simply does not support this idea, and it is becoming increasingly harder to argue that Neolithic Europe was some sort of prehistoric utopia peopled by peace-loving farmers.

I should mention that is well beyond the scope of this book to provide a comprehensive account of all the possible archaeological data pertaining to Neolithic warfare in Europe, and indeed, this would surely be an impossible task entailing the examination of a huge corpus of academic literature written in many different European languages. I have therefore had to be selective in what is included in its pages and not all of Europe has been covered, although all of the famous sites connected with Neolithic warfare have been included, along with some that are not so well known. It should also be noted that some of the archaeological material covered here dates to the period that is often referred to as the Chalcolithic, Copper, or Early Bronze Age, when copper (and gold) objects first began to be made and used in Europe. However, the Copper Age communities of Europe were, to all intents and purposes, still living a Neolithic lifestyle. Hence the reason why many archaeologists prefer to use the terms Late Neolithic, Final Neolithic, or Eneolithic, for this fascinating and hugely important time of transition.

Of course, some people may wonder why we would want to study warfare in prehistory? After all, it has caused human societies so much pain and suffering, with millions of people killed around the globe as the result of warfare, and unfortunately, as we are all too aware, this ugliest facet of human nature shows no signs of going away. However, to quote Don Brothwell: 'A first obvious answer is that there is plenty of evidence in the past of weapons and direct evidence of human trauma indicative of some form of conflict. But more importantly, human aggression, conflict and warfare have a history, and archaeology demonstrates that the temporal dimension is long and deserves detailed study, as it is certainly a major and recurring theme in ancient human society'.[2] Taking a similar view Helle Vankilde says: 'Archaeology clearly has the potential to provide knowledge about the evolutionary position of warfare in a deep historical perspective, warfare's possible role as a primary mover, and other topical issues, but it is a scientific venture only just begun'.[3] Of course, while such arguments are hard to disagree with, we must also remember that behind the mute archaeological remains covered in this book, there are human stories of grief, pain, and suffering.

Was it War?

There is considerable academic debate as to whether the armed conflicts that undoubtedly took place in Neolithic Europe, actually represent 'true' or 'real' warfare, and some archaeologists consider that is was not until the Bronze Age that such warfare emerged.[4] For others, 'authentic' warfare begins much further forward in time with the emergence of the state and its professional armies. The idea that only states make war has long been a feature of western philosophy, and this idea can be traced back to the Athenian general and historian Thucydides (c. 460–395 BC): Thucydides catergorised war as the ultimate use of force to achieve political goals, and this idea has been favoured by scholars for over two millennia.

Perhaps the most famous of these scholars was the Prussian general Carl von Clausewitz (1780–1831 AD) whose famous military treatise *On War* (1832), is still widely studied today by military historians and strategists, with his theories influencing later renowned military leaders such as the American generals, Dwight D. Eisenhower and George S. Patton. This association of 'true' or 'real' war with the state continues to permeate both archaeological and anthropological thinking, but it has been plausibly argued that no real distinction should be made between the conflicts fought by pre-state and state-led societies: 'states are political units waging war, as local groups in societies without a state are, and the logic and dynamics of war between states are, despite all the differences between 'primitive' and 'civilised' war, comparable to those in war between local groups'.[5]

Ultimately, what actually constitutes 'true' war and whether it was a feature of life in the European Neolithic, comes down to personal opinion and how one interprets the undeniable evidence for lethal armed conflicts that exists from this profoundly important period of later prehistory. In this book, however, I am going to follow Patricia Lambert who has defined war as 'a state or period of armed hostility existing between politically auton-omous units'.[6] This definition provides a useful theoretical framework in which to study Neolithic warfare, for as Lambert further notes, 'it is inclu-sive and does not discriminate between small-scale forms of engagement, such as raiding, ambush, and surprise attacks, that tend to characterize tribal warfare'.[7] As European Neolithic society would also have been tribal in nature, then it seems likely that the warfare that broke out amongst Europe's first farming communities was similar in nature to the small-scale warfare documented by anthropologists around the world. However, we should be wary of equating 'small-scale' with 'ineffective' or 'of little importance', as numerous ethnographic accounts clearly show that tribal warfare was often very savage, and that it could also have a considerable impact on the social equilibrium of non-state or 'primitive' societies. In fact, it can reasonably be argued that the warfare of non-state societies was just as brutal, destructive, and deadly, as the wars waged by both ancient and modern states.

The most common and deadly form of non-state warfare was the raid, which – unsurprisingly – would often take place at night or dawn, when enemies would be more likely to be caught unawares. Franz Boas recorded one such raid on America's Northwest Coast, where fortified villages were frequently raided and levelled in tribal wars: 'The enemy was attacked early in the morning, when it was still dark...The attacking party rarely met with resistance, because they always tried to surprise the enemy while asleep...When the men were killed, their heads were cut off with their war axes. They burned the village. Women who pleased the warriors, and children, were taken as slaves'.[8] Boas does not tell us what happened to the women and children who were not taken as slaves, but one suspects that their lives did not end peacefully. Napoleon Chagnon, who lived with, and documented the lives of the famously warlike Yanomamö/Yanomami peo-ple of Venezuela/Brazil, recorded that the village in which he resided was raided about twenty-five times by a dozen different groups, over a fifteen month period. Most Yanomamö raids ended after a few individuals were killed, but incessant raiding such as that recorded by Chagnon could force people to abandon their villages for other friendly ones, with the houses and gardens of these deserted villages then destroyed by the victorious enemy group.

Further evidence for the brutality of non-state warfare comes from the New Guinea highlands (an area also well-known for its frequent tribal warfare), where a war broke out because of an accusation that a man had died as the result of sorcery practised by a rival group. In the ensuing hostilities, men, women, and children were burnt alive in their homes, and the victors drove the vanquished from their territory. There is also the early ethnographic account of William Buckley, a British convict who escaped from the ship that brought him to Australia in the early nineteenth century, to live with an Aboriginal tribe for two years: 'The contests between the Watouronga, of Geelong, and the Warrorongs, of the Yarra, were fierce and bloody. I have accompanied the former in their attacks on the latter. When coming suddenly upon them in the night, they have destroyed without mercy men, women and children'.[9] In Tahitian warfare, women and children could also suffer greatly, as there are accounts of enemy children being pinned to their mothers with spears. In New Zealand, female captives were sometimes intentionally disabled by warriors, leaving them unable to escape, and permitting the warriors to rape, kill or eat them whenever they desired.

Various Euro-American accounts dating from the sixteenth to nineteenth centuries (not all of which were biased against 'heathen savages' and thus untruthful) have provided evidence of the terrible treatment that could be meted out to male war captives of the famous Iroquois Confederacy (comprising the Seneca, Cayuga, Onondaga, Oneida, and Mohawk tribes). One captured warrior would be selected and given the 'honour' of a ritual execution. Before he was killed the selected individual would be allowed to hold a death feast in the village where he was being held captive, during which he was saluted by his executioners, and also allowed to recount his war exploits and honours. On the day of his execution the individual would be tied to a stake and burned from the feet up with firebrands and other red-hot objects by villagers, men, women, and children. He was then scalped, with hot sand thrown on to his exposed skull, finally being put out of his misery with a knife to the chest or a tomahawk to the head. The flesh would then be stripped from his bones and cooked in large war kettles, with all of the villagers participating in the 'feast'.

Archaeological evidence from the Arctic region of the North Pacific Rim also presents a picture of tribal life that is far removed from the equitable and harmonious one that some people still like to eulogise over. In fact, archaeological evidence from this region suggests that previous to the arrival of the first Russians and Europeans, warfare had been a feature of life for several thousands of years, and played a critical role in the development of north Pacific society.[10] Some of the most graphic evidence for prehistoric warfare in the North Pacific Rim was found at the Saunaktuk site located in the Mackenzie Delta of the Canadian Northwest territories. The remains of at least thirty-five Inuit who had died in the late fourteenth century AD were discovered here, and 68 per cent of the dead were children with the majority of the others old men and women. These remains clearly revealed extreme levels of violence with knife cuts, slash wounds, evidence of facial muti- lation, and decapitation, present on the bones, and some people had very probably been tortured before they were killed. Some of the long bones had also been split, quite possibly revealing the extraction of marrow for human consumption. It may well be the case that the massacre at the site was carried out while most of the younger men of the community were away hunting, as native oral tradition records.

The casualties of war could also be extremely high in tribal warfare. For example, in British Columbia, four hundred members of the Lilloet tribe were lost in raids carried out by an enemy tribe over the course of a week, which effectively meant that some 10 per cent of their population was wiped out as a result. Similarly, in a raid that took place during an episode of war- fare in the Happy Valley region of New Guinea, 125 people from an alliance of tribes were killed, representing 6.2 per cent of the population of this large group. Amongst the Waorani of the Ecuadorian Amazon, over 60 per cent of adult deaths over five generations were related to feuding and warfare, while a study of twenty-eight non-state societies, revealed that most of them killed captured enemy warriors, and that one-fourth of these societies also killed captured enemy non-combatants (i.e. women and children). In fact, it is rather sobering to learn that in relative terms, the number of people killed in non-state warfare was much higher than in the ones waged by states (20–30 per cent in the former and some 5 per cent in the latter).

There are also many ethnographic accounts of tribal societies engaging in formal pitched battles that were more ritualised or ceremonial in nature, and which were more to do with aggressive posturing rather than actually killing enemy warriors. However, we should not lose sight of the fact that although limited, there were nevertheless sometimes serious casualties in these encounters, and they could also escalate into full-blown conflicts with many people losing their lives, with settlements attacked and destroyed. In the

New Guinea highlands, these battles were prearranged (as they often were elsewhere) and basically involved opposing lines of warriors throwing arrows or spears from behind their shields, with noisy insults and challenges flying back and forth between the two lines, which would be just within killing range of one another. The relatively low casualty rates of these New Guinean ceremonial battles led the Maring clan to refer to them as 'small fights' or 'nothing fights'. Similar battles were documented amongst the famous Great Plains Indians of North America and we have a fascinating late 18th century account of one such battle from a native Cree named Saukamapee:

'Both parties made a great show of their numbers...After some singing and dancing they sat down on the ground, and placed their large shields before them...their arrows went a long way and whizzed about as balls do from guns...Our iron-headed arrows did not go through their shields, but stuck in them. On both sides, several were wounded, but none lay on the ground; and night put an end to the battle, without a scalp being taken on either side.'[11]

Battles such as these led earlier anthropologists such as Quincy Wright and Harry Turney-High (who published the influential works *A Study of War* (1942) and *Primitive War* (1949) respectively) to the conclusion that tribal warfare was little more than a deadly game, which had little impact on 'primitive' societies. However, as we have seen from the ethnographic accounts of tribal warfare above (and bearing in mind that there are many more similar ones), such conclusions are clearly wrong.

Identifying Neolithic Warfare

As in other prehistoric or more recent, non-state societies around the world, the most obvious signs of Neolithic warfare are intentional or malevolent, unhealed perimortem injuries (occurring at or near the time of death) seen on skeletons, and arrows embedded in bones provide an obvious and well documented example. Of course, healed ante-mortem injuries (received before death), such as parry fractures seen on forearm bones, which can also be seen on many Neolithic skeletons, may also be an indication of warfare, the only difference being that they may represent lucky escapes. As we will see, some of the Neolithic skeletal or osteological evidence included in this book, speaks of acts of warfare that 'went beyond the pale', and also of battles probably involving hundreds of combatants. Undoubtedly, it should be borne in mind that some of this evidence very probably represents acts of interpersonal violence (i.e. homicide, brawls), execution of criminals, or even accidents, rather than actual warfare. However, even with these caveats in mind, it still seems likely that a good deal of these injuries were received in the warfare that broke out between European Neolithic communities. In fact, many traumatic injuries have been identified on Neolithic skeletons from sites across Europe and form the main subject of the excellent *Sticks, Stones, and Broken Bones: Neolithic Violence in a European Perspective*. Some of the skeletal evidence covered in detail within its pages (some of which is mentioned in this book) would certainly be an eye-opener for those who still delude themselves that Europe's first farming communities essentially followed a peaceful existence and had little time for violence and warfare.

We might also wonder about the unrecognised victims of Neolithic warfare in Europe. Although writing about prehistoric warfare in North America, the arguments of George Milner are of undoubted relevance in this regard: 'The bodies of people who died far away from the village would not always have been found and returned for burial, particularly if the deaths took place deep in enemy territory. For victims interred in village cemeteries, it is by no means sure that their violent deaths would be detected because lethal wounds often do not leave distinctive marks on bones. Incomplete skeletons and poor bone preservation further reduce the recognition of casualties'.[12] Furthermore, all too often, archaeologists turn to the idea that the human bones that they find in the ditches of Neolithic enclosures and tombs are evidence of ancestral rituals rather than possible indicators of violence and warfare. We should also remember that there would have been living victims of Neolithic warfare, as people would have lost loved ones, had their homes and even villages destroyed, and in some cases, were probably driven from their tribal territories. Forced 'migrations' such as these may also have led to the deaths of the very young and old, and those people who were dangerously sick.

In recent years, there has also been a growing acceptance that many of the flint arrowheads previously identified as grave goods in European Neolithic tombs, actually entered these tombs in the bodies of people they had killed. In fact, these arrows are often found with snapped-off tips, revealing that they had hit something solid – like a human body. It is also interesting to note the results of Milner's study of arrow wounds (both lethal and non-lethal), mainly received by soldiers in the war fought between the native Americans and the U.S. Army in 1900, which indicated that only about one in three arrows damaged bone.[13] In fact, archaeological evidence from Europe in general, reveals that for the most part, it was Neolithic men who were killed by arrows, indicating armed conflicts or archery battles between different male groups using bows. It may be possible, that as in the medieval period,

Neolithic boys were taught archery from a young age to prepare them for the armed conflicts that might await them in manhood.

Many Neolithic people may also have died as the result of relatively minor wounds received in warfare that subsequently led to untreatable lethal infections. Although Neolithic communities in Europe would have had their own range of plant-based medicines, without modern medicine and surgery, they must surely have been at a disadvantage when it came to treating war wounds, just as soldiers of earlier historical armies were. In fact, arrow and other wounds that were not initially life-threatening would be fertile breeding grounds for tetanus spores, and in many cases lethal blood poisoning would have ensued as a result of these wounds.

It is also quite possible that some Neolithic groups also enhanced the lethality of their projectile weapons by applying poisons to them just as more recent tribal peoples are known to have done. For example, North American Indians and the ancient Sarmatians (c. 600 BC–450 AD) of the Russian steppes both used snake venom to poison their arrows, and poisoned arrows have also been found in some ancient Egyptian tombs. There is also circumstantial evidence that poisoned arrows were used to kill people in Chinese Neolithic warfare.

Archaeologists also other draw on other main lines of evidence when identifying the presence of prehistoric warfare in the archaeological record. These are: settlement data (e.g. fortifications in the form of substantial walls and ditches, evidence of attack and destruction of settlements), war weaponry, and iconography.

Although there is something of an archaeological tendency to view Neolithic walls and ditches as expressions of status or as a ritual and ceremonial enclosures, it is worth noting that fortified settlements were built by many non-state agricultural societies in other parts of the world. The $p\overline{a}$ of the Maori provide a well-known example, and were first documented by Captain James Cook during his circumnavigation of the North and South Islands. The $p\overline{a}$ were mainly located on the North Island and Cook described the coastal $p\overline{a}$ at Wharekaho, Mercury Bay. This featured a ditch 3 m deep cutting off the headland, with a palisade comprising logs just over 3 m tall. An earthwork fighting platform was also constructed against its inner side, allowing its defenders to rain down stones and other missiles on any enemy forces. Many of the palisade posts often reached 7–9 m high and their tops were carved with fearsome human heads with gnashing teeth and protruding tongues. These palisades cannot have been a particularly welcoming site for any attacking force.

Archaeology has also revealed that some of the non-state fortified settlements of the New World obviously met a violent end, with some of the best
evidence in this respect found at villages and towns of the Native American
Mississippian Culture (c. 1000–1600 AD) in the Central Illinois River Valley.
In this region, palisaded settlements were strategically located on low bluffs
or hills (c. 40–45 m high) that commanded good views of the surrounding
countryside. This, however, did not stop them from being attacked, and it is
evident that several met their end as a result of enemy assaults, with some
also being torched and burnt to the ground. Possible evidence for one such
assault was found at the site of Orendorf, a fairly large Middle Mississippian
village (c. 1150–1250 AD) located on the northern edge of the Central
Illinois River Valley. Part of the settlement mound was excavated and around
twenty-five of the c. 268 skeletons were found to display warfare-related
trauma comprising embedded projectile points, evidence of scalping and
decapitation, and skull fractures and facial wounds. These people (and perhaps others from the mortuary sample) may indeed have been killed during
an attack on Orendorf, but it is also possible that they were killed whilst away
from the village.

In contrast to the obvious military paraphernalia (e.g. swords and shields)
of the succeeding Bronze and Iron Ages, it is harder to identify specialised weapons of war in the Neolithic, as it is clear that in Neolithic warfare,
people often used what archaeologists refer to as 'tool-weapons' to dispatch
their enemies. The ubiquitous stone axe of the Neolithic provides us with
an obvious example, for although they would have been vital to early farming communities for tasks such as woodland clearance and carpentry, as we
will see in this book, they were also clearly used as deadly killing weapons.
It is also worth bearing in mind that the ethnographic record is replete with
examples of wooden war clubs, such as the ball-headed clubs used by the
Native American Iroquois and Algonquian tribes, the knobkerries used by
the famous Zulu and other African tribes, or the Totokia used in Fijian tribal
warfare. That similar weapons existed in the Neolithic seems likely, such as
the two wooden Neolithic clubs that were found along with a stone axe with
preserved beech-wood haft, at Ehenside Tarn, in Cumbria (Fig. 1). Wooden
spears tipped with (or without) flint and bone points could also have been
used in warfare as well as in hunting, and there have been rare finds of these
weapons in Europe (e.g. the c. 2 m long example made from hazel, which
was discovered in Somerset near the famous Neolithic trackway known
as the 'Sweet Track'). Many scholars argue that it was not until the Late
Neolithic/Chalcolithic that specific weapons of war appeared, with objects

such as stone mace-heads or barbed and tanged aarrow-heads cited in this respect (Fig. 2). However, such weapons were also arguably present in the earlier Neolithic, and in fact, many of the flint arrow-heads made during the whole of the European Neolithic were arguably made with warfare more in mind, rather than hunting. This is suggested by the general scarcity of wild animals at Neolithic settlement (and ritual) sites across Europe, with domesticated animals dominating bone assemblages.

As will be seen in the course of this book, all of these archaeological indicators of warfare are present in the European Neolithic. However, these signs of war should not be taken as evidence that the first farming communities of Europe were constantly living in its bloody shadow. As Mike Parker Pearson rightly warns us, we need to wary of letting the theoretical pendulum swing the other way, and of seeing prehistoric warfare everywhere, just because there has rightly been a backlash against the politically correct, 'pacified past'.[14] Similarly, Martin Smith has pointed out that the evidence for Neolithic warfare 'should not be overplayed or we risk creating a vision of an anarchic and brutalised prehistory that may be just as inaccurate as the rose-tinted idyll which preceded it'.[15] Nonetheless, even bearing these caveats in mind, archaeological evidence (which continues to accumulate) from across Europe, clearly reveals that warfare was not a rare occurrence in the Neolithic. It is also obvious that at times, this warfare involved extreme levels of violence, with men, women, and children killed indiscriminately.

The Causes of Neolithic Warfare: Some Suggestions

We can obviously never know the true story of what fuelled warfare in Neolithic Europe, but by the time of the Early Neolithic (if not earlier) there would have been territories and resources to fight over. Two Neolithic resources that spring immediately to mind are livestock and grain, which would have formed the main subsistence base for many European Neolithic communities. However, it would have been cattle that were more vulnerable to the depredations of Neolithic war parties, as grain (and other crops) would have been stored inside Neolithic houses and settlements, whereas cattle and other livestock would have been a source of mobile wealth that would have been easier to steal away during raids. In fact, some Neolithic enclosures of Europe, which show strong evidence for fortification, may well have been built as a defence against such cattle raiding, which has been widely recorded amongst non-state societies in the ethnographic record. For example, the Nyangatom people who live along the southern border

of Ethiopia and South Sudan, and who are still involved in ongoing conflicts with other groups such as the Turkana and Suri, conduct two types of
raid: stealth raids comprising small groups of warriors (4–25), who attempt
to capture poorly guarded cattle from enemy settlements, and battle raids
which commonly involve hundreds of warriors, who aim to capture livestock
by force, or to attack and annihilate enemy groups. Of course, cattle may not
have been the only source of wealth that drove attacks on Neolithic enclosures, as it is evident that many examples formed focal points in complex
trade and exchange networks along which raw materials and finished products passed such as flint, salt, pottery, and polished stone axes, would have
passed. Control of these sites and the materials accumulated within them
would have led to greater power in Neolithic society, and in some cases, such
sites probably proved too tempting a target for individuals and communities
who had previously cast a covetous gaze over them.

In some cases, two-legged rather than four-legged booty may have been
the objective of Neolithic raiding parties, as the practice of slavery has
been shown to have a long and terrible history in human society. Of course,
this does not therefore mean that we can automatically assume that slavery was also a part of life in Neolithic Europe. However, it is nevertheless
quite conceivable that some raids on Neolithic settlements in Europe were
carried out in order to acquire captives, who could then be exploited for
whatever purpose. In fact, as will be seen later, possible evidence for the capture of women and children has been found at sites of the famous Neolithic
Linearbandkeramik (LBK) Culture in Germany. In many non-state societies, women captured in warfare were also seen as symbols of success that
enhanced the status and prestige of their owners, and raids were often conducted with the sole purpose of capturing females. These captured women
would then either become slaves, concubines, secondary or full spouses, or
in some cases, were ransomed off to the community they had originally been
stolen from.

The ethnographic record also suggests that it would not have just been
land and other resources that fuelled warfare in Neolithic Europe, and
that sometimes, attacks on other communities were driven by less prosaic
motives. In fact, one of the commonest causes of violence and warfare in
non-state societies was blood revenge, and we have already seen an example
of this with the episode of warfare in New Guinea, which was sparked by a
death perceived to have been caused by the malevolent sorcery of another
group. Although these revenge raids sought to dispatch the original member of the other community who had been responsible for the killing, any

member of this community would be 'fair game' and could be killed. More importantly, these revenge killings often set in motion a chain of tit-for-tat killings between rival groups, which subsequently escalated into actual full-scale warfare. For instance, Napoleon Chagnon recorded that in 1965, the headman of a Yanomamö village was murdered in retaliation for an earlier killing, and that in turn, this led to a series of revenge raids on the offending group, which were still being carried out ten years after his death. Wayne Lee has also noted in his discussion of native warfare in the eastern woodlands of North America, that the difficulty with 'blood revenge' is that the war party who were mobilised for this reason, would more commonly comprise young men looking to enhance their status by the taking of as many enemy scalps and prisoners as possible.[16] Thus it would often be the case that those communities who had been on the receiving end of such treatment would respond in kind, with the original act of blood revenge subsequently becoming lost in a vicious and self-perpetuating cycle of raids and counter-raids. Many other examples of 'revenge warfare' could be cited such as that recorded amongst the Kofyar people of northern Nigeria. Some of these Kofyar armed conflicts could also carry on sporadically for many years, such as the one recorded as having lasted from 1902–1925. This conflict was initially triggered by the mysterious death of a boy that was deemed to have been a murder carried out by another group, and which led to several (documented) deaths and the destruction of some villages.

Sometimes, it may simply have been 'fear of the other' that forced the Neolithic communities of Europe to attack each other. In non-state societies, a dominant centralised power or state was lacking, and thus there were no systems of law to prevent any group who wished to do so, from launching an attack on another group at any time. Azar Gat has called this unstable state of affairs in non-state societies, 'the security dilemma', with communities forced to launch pre-emptive strikes against potential enemies who could be likewise preparing to attack them. As Gat says: 'When the other must be regarded as a potential enemy, his very existence poses a threat, for he might suddenly attack one day'.[17]

The 'Pacification' of the Neolithic

For much of the later twentieth century, it would be fair to say that warfare was only given a bit-part, or even written out of the story of Neolithic Europe. Indeed, this was something I realised as an Archaeology student at the University of Liverpool, with the academic texts on the Neolithic that

I studied giving short shrift to the subject, instead concentrating on more 'peaceful' aspects of life such as trade and religion. The clear instances of lethal armed conflict and other possible evidence for Neolithic warfare were admittedly not ignored, but they were downplayed and not given the attention I felt that they arguably deserved. This shunting of warfare to the sidelines in European Neolithic studies is perhaps a little puzzling, particularly given that the evidence for it was certainly not lacking. However, the 'pacification' of the Neolithic may well be related to a social response by Western society who had lived through the horrors of the First and Second Word Wars. Not surprisingly, people would have wanted to forget the death and destruction they had witnessed as a result of these terrible global conflicts, with academics largely turning their backs on the evidence for European prehistoric warfare in general. It is true that warfare was not totally consigned to the academic wilderness, but neither was it really seen as a significant aspect of life that could ruin and destroy lives, and something which could also affect the trajectory of societal development.

In fact, this later twentieth century pacification of prehistoric Europe was seriously challenged as a result of the publication of Keeley's seminal book, *War Before Civilization: The Myth of the Peaceful Savage*.[18] There can be no doubting the influence of this important publication on archaeological thinking, and many prehistorians were turned from 'doves' to 'hawks' because of its publication. I have to admit that like many others, I found it a persuasive book in regard to its central tenet – i.e. that for the most part, both anthropologists and archaeologists had been guilty of casting the past in a largely peaceful light. Although *War Before Civilization* has not been free from criticism, with some accusing Keely of rhetoric and over-exaggeration, there can be little doubt that its publication marked an important turning point in warfare studies in both archaeology and anthropology. At the least, it forced academics from both disciplines to accept that both ancient and more recent non-state peoples were far more violent and bellicose than they had often been portrayed previously. It is also worth noting that over ten years before the publication of *War Before Civilization*, Slavomil Vencl had written an important paper entitled *War and Warfare* in *Archaeology*.[19] In this important article, Vencl essentially argues that it was unlikely that prehistoric Europe had developed along peaceful lines, and that archaeologists had presented a distorted vision of prehistory by not taking into account the impact of warfare on its various societies.

Interestingly, Keeley's book emerged during very troubled times, and just as the horrors of World Wars I and II probably pushed prehistoric warfare to the side-lines in narratives on European prehistory, events at the end of the twentieth century may well have played their part in placing this darker side of human society on the archaeological agenda. In fact, it is quite possible, if not likely, that the wars, genocides, and break-up of nation-states that took place in several places around the world during this time, led to a growing archaeological and anthropological interest in warfare in general. The mass media coverage of these events also made it impossible to ignore them, and, as a result, archaeologists may also have been forced to confront the violent reality of life in prehistoric Europe.

I am sure some academic eyebrows will be raised in exasperation at another book on prehistoric warfare. Nevertheless, is a book that I have wanted to write for some time, but which has been side-lined because of other projects. Its roots can probably be traced back to my childhood, when like many young boys, I became fascinated by war, and in particular, the conflicts of the First and Second World Wars. However, it was only several years later that I became aware that warfare had a much more ancient heritage reaching back at least as far as the Neolithic, if not beyond, as there is certainly evidence for lethal armed conflict in both the Palaeolithic and Mesolithic (the 'Old' and 'Middle' Stone Ages respectively). As we will see in the following chapters, although Kipling may have mixed up the Palaeolithic with the Neolithic (woolly horses were extinct by the Neolithic and the 'Dawn of Man' lay much further back in the past than the time of the Europe's first farmers), he appears to have been right about the 'savage war' that was waged during this profound turning point in the human story.

Chapter 1

The Earliest Evidence for European Neolithic Warfare: Greece and the Balkans

G reece is a country that has long been famed for its ancient warfare. For example, many readers will be familiar with the semi-mythical Bronze Age warfare of Homer's *Iliad*, the warfare of the Classical Greek city-states (*Poleis*) with its formidable Hoplite infantrymen, or the heroic resistance of the Spartan king, Leonidas, and his vastly outnumbered army at the pass of Thermopylae. But is there any evidence to suggest that the Neolithic farming communities of Greece also engaged in warfare? The answer to this question is yes. However, some would beg to differ, as although attitudes are beginning to change as a result of the evidence coming out of other parts of Europe, to some extent, there is still something of an archaeological reluctance to acknowledge Greek Neolithic warfare. This is probably understandable given that in comparison to other parts of Europe, the evidence for Neolithic warfare in Greece is perhaps somewhat ambiguous. Nevertheless, it has been argued – on the basis of the archaeological evidence found here – that there is strong circumstantial evidence for warfare in Neolithic Thessaly at least, and that it would be somewhat odd if warfare did not exist in Neolithic Greece at all.[1] Indeed, as we will see, it is not just in Thessaly that we arguably have 'circumstantial' evidence for Greek Neolithic warfare.

It could also be possible that Thessalian Neolithic warfare was similar to that which occurred in the American south-west prior to European contact, as this huge region had environmental and cultural conditions similar to those seen in Thessaly. This rich archaeological 'laboratory', which has been a training ground for many American archaeologists, was home to the famous Anasazi people, whose later sites (c. 1240–1300 AD) have produced some of the best evidence for prehistoric warfare in general. This warfare seems to have been sparked by a series of droughts that began in the latter half of the twelfth century, and which increasingly got worse in the thirteenth century, leading to a lack of resources for a growing population. By the mid-13th century, serious warfare had come to the Anasazi region, as revealed by the burned and destroyed houses, people killed by arrows, and decapitated individuals found at several Anasazi sites from this time. Evidence of scalping and cannibalism has also been noted on Anasazi skeletons, with people perhaps being driven to eat each other because of starvation. Undoubtedly, the most impressive reminder of Anasazi warfare are the remarkable cliff-top dwellings that were built high up on steep mesas in remote canyons. Many survive to this day in superb and somewhat ghostly states of preservation, appearing as though their inhabitants have only just abandoned them (Fig. 3).

Analysis of the distribution of Neolithic settlements in Thessaly also suggests that as in the American South-West, these settlements were separated by empty territory.[2] In the latter region, no-man's-lands were necessary buffer zones that separated groups of that were at war with one another, or who at the least, wished to distance themselves from potential enemies

Greek Cave Burials: Evidence of Warfare?

As was the case with many other Neolithic communities in Europe, those who lived in Greece used caves as burial places. Although caves would have provided convenient areas for the disposal of the dead, it is more likely that people were often buried in them for spiritual rather than practical reasons. Numerous ethnographic accounts from around the world have shown how many societies have viewed (and still view) caves as sacred places that provide portals or doorways to the supernatural world. Whatever the reasoning behind Greek Neolithic cave burials, human remains recovered from some examples display injuries that may point towards outbreaks of warfare.

Perhaps the most intriguing of these remains are those recovered from Alepotrypa Cave, which is located at Diros Bay on the Tainaron Peninsula of southern Greece. This important and impressive site was discovered in 1958, and the subsequent excavations that have taken place here since 1970 have uncovered much fascinating evidence relating to life at the cave during the latter stages of the Neolithic c. 5000–3200 BC (e.g. flint and obsidian tools, marble and clay figurines, copper daggers, clay ovens, and numerous domesticated animal bones). Hundreds of people may well have lived in the cave at any one time, as it covers an area roughly the size of four football pitches.

There were two main burial areas in the cave, and the remains of at least 161 people were recovered, with people interred in multiple and single burials (a small, discrete corner of the cave also contained two child cremation burials). From our perspective, the most interesting aspect of this skeletal material is that small, circular (sometimes multiple) depressed fractures feature on 13 per cent of the skulls. All of these fractures had healed before death and were found on the skulls of males, females, and older children. These fractures may indicate non-lethal ritual combat carried out in order to reslove various disputes. Such combat is not uncommon among tribal peoples, with the stick or machete fights (the non-cutting edges of machetes were used) fights of the Yanamamö Indians providing a well-known example. Similarly, among the Surma people of southern Sudan and south-western Ethiopia, stick fighting is known as *donga* or *saginay* and often takes place between two men seeking the same bride. Occasionally, however, as is the case elsewhere with non-lethal ritual combat, deaths have occasionally occurred during these Yanamamö and Surma ritual fights.

Healed depressed fractures reminiscent of those from Alepotrypa Cave have been documented not only on other Neolithic European skulls (e.g. those found in British Neolithic tombs), but also on those recovered from ancient sites in the New World. For example, numerous healed fractures have been recorded on Chumash Indian skulls from southern California, and also on those recovered from sites of the Chinchorro people of northern Chile. It has been suggested that injuries seen on the Chinchorro skulls may point towards violent mock fights involving the throwing of stones, which were carried out during funerary rituals.[3] Alternatively, it could be that the trauma seen on skulls is related to disputes over harvesting and hunting grounds, the procurement of mates, or other personal arguments that had become over-heated and needed resolving. Whatever caused this Chinchorro cranial trauma, the fact that a quartz projectile point was also found embedded in the spine of one individual, indicates that not all Chinchorro fights were non-lethal, ritualised affairs.

Although it is perhaps more likely that the fractures seen on the Neolithic skulls from Alepotrypa Cave were received in ritual fights involving stones, clubs or sticks, we must also consider the possibility that sling bullets caused these fractures. It has been noted that the stone and clay sling bullets commonly found on Neolithic Greek sites (e.g. caches of sling bullets have been found at Sesklo, Rakhmani and Tsangli) are of a similar size, shape, and weight, as those used in the warfare of the later Classical period.[4] Not all would agree that Neolithic sling bullets were weapons of war, however. Catherine Perlès, for example, has argued that the clay sling bullets at least would not have been suitable in this respect, as they would have been too light and fragile for use in war, and that it is more likely that as in parts of the modern Near East, they were used by shepherds to control wandering sheep.[5] However, it has been pointed out that in the Neolithic Near East, similar sling bullets are fairly common in archaeological contexts associated with the attack and destruction of settlements, and are also known from the destruction levels noted at some Greek Early Bronze Age settlements.[6] It could be reasonably argued, then, that Greek Neolithic sling bullets were indeed a weapon of war used in the attack and defence of the earliest farming settlements in Greece.

The multiple burial of eight people that was found in Alepotrypa Cave, which comprises both young adults and children, should also be mentioned here. These people seem to have been buried rather haphazardly, and, a number of bones were also missing from their skeletons. One individual had been buried lying face down in an extended position, and although there were no signs of violence evident on the skeletons, the possibility remains that the individuals in this burial were violently killed, as a lack of traumatic injuries does not necessarily equal a peaceful death. Also, the skull of an individual found at Alepotrypa Cave is said to have displayed a large, unhealed wound. However, this skull has unfortunately since gone missing, and thus the nature and severity of this wound remain unknown.

Also of interest are discoveries made at the cemetery associated with the Late Neolithic settlement of Kephala in the Aegean Islands (over sixty skeletons were found, representing one of the largest and best-preserved Neolithic mortuary samples from Greece). A partially healed injury was noted on a male skull found in the cemetery, which took the form of a small hole, 8 x 11 mm in size that was surrounded by a healed depression with cuts around it. It may be that this depression is related to the removal of some sort of projectile point. If so, it seemed that the man had survived this probable projectile wound for some time, although eventually, it probably became fatally infected. Also found at the cemetery was a grave containing two adult males who do not appear to have been accorded much respect when they died. One man was laid on his front with his leg bent towards his head, the other lay on his back, his legs bent under his body. The positions of both bodies suggest that the dead men were simply dropped in the grave, and the fact that they are also likely to have been buried very shortly after they died (probably within twelve hours) strengthens the case for violent rather than peaceful death. Another adult male skull from Kephala appears to have suffered from a head wound, probably caused by a blade of some sort. It is also interesting to note that two holes had been drilled into both parietal bones (the bones forming the sides and roof of the skull) after the man's death, suggesting that it may have been hung up and displayed somewhere in the settlement. Another possible casualty of war was found at the famous Early Neolithic settlement of Neo Nikomedeia in central Macedonia, a site which has yielded a wealth of evidence pertaining to the lives of Greece's first farmers. The body of a young man was recovered from one of the graves found at the site. Curiously, he had a large polished stone between his teeth, but of more interest was the serious wound on his skull, which could indicate that he died in violent circumstances.

Dimini and Sesklo: Fortified Sites?

As is the case elsewhere in Europe, there are Neolithic settlements in Greece that have architectural features which are arguably defensive in nature. Those found at the famous 'tell' sites of Dimini and Sesklo in Thessaly providing us with an obvious starting point. Tells are the characteristic settlement of the Greek and Balkan Neolithic and originate in the Neolithic Near East, although 'flat' settlements lacking the tells or mounds that built up as the result of successive episodes of habitation, are also known.

Initially excavated between 1899 and 1906 by Christos Tsountas, Dimini and Sesklo were the first Neolithic settlements uncovered in Greece, and Tsountas was the first archaeologist to propose they were fortified sites in his classic volume *The Prehistoric Citadels of Dimini and Sesklo* (1908). This idea has since become less popular, but several archaeologists still follow Tsountas, arguing that the evidence favours the idea that both Dimini and Sesklo were defended Neolithic settlements. The two sites are located only a few miles apart near the north-eastern coast of Thessaly, with the former being the more impressive of the two, at least in terms of its possible defensive architecture. Located on a schist outcrop at 18 m above sea level, Dimini was inhabited during the Late Neolithic between c.4800–4500 BC and the settlement (which covers about 1 hectare) basically comprises six or seven stone-walled enclosures that encircle habitation terraces and a central courtyard at the top of a hill on which the remains of a large three-roomed building or 'megaron' were discovered (Fig. 4). This structure may possibly date to the Early Bronze Age, but a comparison with similar buildings found at other Late Neolithic Greek settlements (e.g. Ayia Sophia Magoula, Magoula Visviki, and Sesklo) suggests that this is unlikely. Some archaeologists have – not implausibly – viewed these buildings as the dwelling places of elite families or groups who sat at the head of a stratified Neolithic society, and who controlled agricultural surplus and other products. Of course, it could be possible that these structures were actually communal buildings of some sort used by the whole village. However, the former idea is perhaps more likely, given that the archaeological record of Neolithic Europe supports the idea that there were privileged individuals and groups who were socially elevated above other members of society.

The enclosure walls at Dimini measure c. 1.5 m in width, and although they do not seem to have been particularly high (less than 3 m) we cannot rule out the possibility that they were further heightened by the addition of adobe (mud brick) walls or even wooden palisades. The idea that these possible fortification walls had a defensive function have been challenged by some Greek archaeologists such as George Hourmouziadis, who undertook further excavations at the site in the 1970s. As Dimitra Kokkinidou and Marianna Nikolaidou have noted, Hourmouziadis 'postulated that the encircling walls were designed for organising habitational space and for facilitating craft/industrial pursuits and storage'.[7]

Measuring some 12 hectares in size Sesklo was a substantial settlement inhabited (not continuously) from the Early Neolithic down to the Bronze Age c. 6500–1500 BC. It has been estimated that at its height, its population may perhaps have measured in the low thousands (this estimate has since been revised significantly downwards by some archaeologists into the low hundreds). The site is divided into two separate areas of habitation: the tell or *acropolis* (Sesklo A) excavated by Christos Tsountas in the early twentieth century, and the outlying lower settlement or *polis*, excavated by D.R. Theocharis between 1956–1981. In contrast to the smaller site of Dimini, the possible fortifications at Sesklo are less substantial, with stone walls (c. 1 m in width) enclosing parts of the tell and a central court with megaron, as at Dimini.

As with the Dimini enclosures, the idea that the walls at Sesklo were defensive in nature has since been questioned, with some archaeologists arguing that it is more probable that they functioned as retaining walls, supporting terraces on which the houses were built. However, as the original height of the walls is uncertain, as at the Dimini enclosures, we cannot be sure that those at Sesklo were also not capped with superstructures of some kind, providing a more formidable barrier to any potential enemies.

The counter-arguments against the enclosures at both Dimini and Sesklo are admittedly plausible, and more archaeologists than not now probably favour a non-defensive function for these famous sites. Nonetheless, a closer look at their architecture may suggest otherwise, for the most notable aspect of these enclosures is that they both incorporate baffle gates. Baffle gates are

a characteristic feature of historic and ethnographically documented fortified sites around the world and for example, they were used extensively
in Roman fortifications and were known as *clavicula*. The first European
settlers in the New World also encountered baffle gates incorporated into
native fortifications, in places such as north-eastern America, Africa, and
Mexico. Lawrence Keeley et al. have noted that 'Baffled gates force attackers
who enter them to expose their flanks and rear to defenders' fire. Ideally,
they require attackers to turn left exposing their unshielded right side'.[8]

Interestingly, the baffle gate at Middle Neolithic Sesklo is located on the
western side of the site, which is not 'defended' by the steep ravine that
delimits the eastern part of the settlement. The inhabitants of Dimini also
built baffle gates in both the northern and southern ends of the walls, and a
further two were located in the western quadrant, with a fifth perhaps located
to the south-east. The narrow gateways and corridors that led into the habitation and working areas at Dimini may also have been intended as defensive
features, being put in place to slow down and hinder any potential attackers.

It is perhaps also of some significance that the site of Sesklo shows signs
of extensive burning and destruction, and archaeological evidence from the
Late Neolithic settlement of Pyrgos, which was discovered just 250 m to the
north of Sesklo may also be of some interest to us. The excavation of this site
in 1979 revealed the remains of a small settlement or hamlet comprising a
small cluster of houses, and a thick layer of burnt debris found sandwiched
between two separate archaeological deposits indicated that a fierce fire had
swept through the settlement at some point. Evidence for the deliberate
burning of houses was also discovered during R.J. Rodden's excavations at
Nea Nikomedeia in the 1960s.

In fact, the burning of houses is actually a widespread phenomenon in the
Neolithic of south-eastern Europe in general (and is not uncommon in other
parts of Europe). Archaeologists have argued that this house burning represents a ritualised act marking the end/beginning of the use-life of a house
(perhaps occurring after the head of the household died). Similar arguments
have been put forth in regard to other examples of burnt Neolithic houses
and halls found elsewhere in Europe, such as the impressive examples
uncovered on Dorstone Hill, Herefordshire. However it remains quite pos
sible (if not probable) that some of these houses were actually burnt to the
ground by enemy raiding parties. As we will see below, this certainly seems
to have been the case further to the North in parts of Bulgaria. Of course,
there is also a distinct possibility that many Neolithic houses simply burnt

down by accident, as the materials they were built with (e.g. wood, thatch), would have been very susceptible to accidental fires.

If the people of Dimini and Sesklo did indeed defend themselves by building fortifications, the reason behind their construction can only be speculated upon. However, at Dimini at least, it may have been because some of its inhabitants were in control of the production and exchange of an exotic and 'valuable' (in terms of social power) commodity, which was gazed on with envious eyes by other Neolithic groups in the wider region. This commodity came in the form of personal ornaments (e.g. rings, cylinder beads, and buttons) made from the shells of *spondylus gaederopus* – the European thorny/spiny oyster, which is found in the Mediterranean and Adriatic. It may be, as some experts have argued, that Late Neolithic Dimini was a *spondylus* production centre and was an important hub in a far-reaching trade and exchange network, along which *spondylus* shell ornaments passed. These were exported to other Neolithic communities who lived many miles from Greece and for example, *spondylus* ornaments are often found in graves belonging to people of the famous LBK culture of central and Western Europe, who we will meet again in the next chapter. *Spondylus* ornaments may well have been used by a privileged few to express and manipulate status in Neolithic Greece.

Support for the idea that *Spondylus* ornaments were valued as prestige items in Neolithic Greece, is provided by a rich ethnographic literature. This ethnographic evidence reveals that various objects made from shells were commonly used in social exchanges between different communities, and that these shell ornaments often gave the individuals who acquired, displayed, and circulated them, a greater level of prestige.

Other Possible Fortified Sites in Greece

In addition to Dimini and Sesklo, there are other Greek Neolithic settlements that should be considered as other possible examples of fortified sites. Of undoubted interest in this respect is the extensive Late Neolithic site of Makriyalos/Makrygialos in Piera, northern Greece (Macedonia), which was investigated as a rescue project in advance of road and railway building during the mid-1990s. To date, this project represents the largest Neolithic excavation in Greece and some 6 hectares of a c. 50 hectare site were dug by archaeologists, with a huge wealth of cultural material such as animal bones, carbonised seeds, fine pottery, and clay figurines recovered.

Makriyalos was a non-tell, or 'flat' settlement, and its excavators identi-fied two main phases of occupation (unsurprisingly referred to as Makriyalos I and II), which spanned the later part of the Neolithic c. 5400–4500 BC. Makriyalos I was surrounded by two enclosure ditches (Ditch Alpha and Ditch Beta) and there was a third, but poorly understood ditch (Ditch Beta), which appears to have divided its two counterparts. Alpha was the most impressive enclosure, measuring c. 3.5 m deep and c. 4.5 m wide, its original chain of deeply-dug pits later remodelled to form a continuous ditch with a V-shaped profile. Although somewhat narrow and shallower, in depth, Ditch Beta also had a V-shaped section, and walls of both mud-brick and stone seem to have reinforced the ditches in some parts of the site.

It is possible that the ditches were not defensive in nature, and may sim-ply have been the boundaries of habitation areas, or they may even have been used as refuse dumps or water storage areas. However, it is worth bearing in mind that the digging of a V-shaped ditch is a classic defensive feature used in ancient and more recent fortified sites around the world: 'V or Y-sectioned ditches are impractical for any domestic purpose, as they erode more quickly than any other form and are more difficult to dig, but they represent an ideal form for purposes of defence against human attack, since they offer max-imum exposure of any would-be attacker to defensive projectile fire from above'.[9] The archaeological investigation of Makriyalos also revealed that Ditch Alpha was used as dumping ground for bodies, with the scattered and disarticulated remains of some sixty individuals of all ages casually thrown into the ditch. Although it is not clear how these people died their treatment appears to suggest that those responsible for their burial had little regard for them in death.

Also worthy of note is the site of Strofilas on Andros Island in the Cyclades, where excavations have uncovered a large, Late Neolithic coastal settlement (c. 3800–3200 BC) enclosed by a substantial wall, and which occupies a strategic position in the surrounding landscape. The settlement is located on the western coast of the island at the top of a small peninsula next to a large valley and there are two natural harbours below the settlement. This possible Neolithic fort also commands wide-ranging views across the Aegean Sea, and remarkable evidence of the Neolithic craft that sailed on it has been found in the form of several carvings of boats, which can be seen on the enclosure wall and on rock surfaces elsewhere at the site. The rock carvings of the boats highlight their importance to the Neolithic community, and other rock carvings can also be seen, such as the depictions of jackals hunting deer and a dolphin calf with its mother.

The abundance of fine artefacts found at Strofilas (e.g. tools made from Obsidian and copper ore sources on the island of Melos) indicate that it was an important trading centre occupying a favourable position on Neolithic maritime trade routes, and that it had an important role to play in a wider exchange network along which status goods passed. It thus seems likely that the Neolithic inhabitants of this 'wealthy' site chose its location with care, and further strengthened it with a fortification wall in order to protect their valuable assets – just as the Sesklo community (and other Greek Neolithic communities may have done). In fact, it has rightly been pointed out that there are other Late Neolithic settlements located in parts of the landscape 'that cannot have been selected for their farming potential'.[10] It has also been suggested that we should be paying more attention to the role of warfare in Greek Neolithic society, and the 'dangerous traffic' that may have led people to surround their settlements with probable fortifications.[11]

Several other fortified Greek Neolithic settlements are suspected, such as Mandalo (c. 4500–4000 BC) in western Macedonia. Here, a large field-stone wall some 2.5 m wide and 1.5 m high surrounded the site and there is also evidence to suggest that a second stone wall encircled the settlement. Its location overlooking the surrounding plain may hint that the site had a spe-cial role, and it is quite possible that an élite and powerful group lived here.

Evidence for Neolithic Warfare in Bulgaria

It is likely that some Neolithic houses/settlements in Greece and the rest of Europe were ritually burnt down, or were set on fire accidentally. However, to argue that none were deliberately burnt down in acts of aggression, flies not only in the face of reason, but also in the face of archaeological evidence recovered from Late Neolithic tells (c. 4900–4000 BC) in parts of Bulgaria. Turning first to north-eastern Bulgaria, archaeologists working here have revealed that life here during the fifth millennium B.C. was not exactly peaceful.

It is evident that in this part of Bulgaria at the beginning of the fifth millennium BC, there was a marked and sudden shift in settlement patterns, with communities founding tells in locations that were arguably defensive in nature (e.g. headlands and temporarily flooded areas). Perhaps even more telling are the wattle-and-daub walls (at least some of these had ditches front-ing them) that were erected around these tells. These walls were strength-ened with substantial posts measuring some 0.40 m wide on average, and to judge from the depth of the deeply-dug holes (0.50–0.80 m in depth) that had held these long-since rotted posts, they originally reached around 3 m in height. These palisades were also arranged in multiple lines, forming rectangular enclosures around the houses in which these Late Neolithic tell communities lived. It could be that these enclosures were erected by migrants in order to protect themselves against possible aggression from local groups. However, there are no clear signs that these settlements were ever assaulted by enemy forces, but this does not mean that warfare was non–existent, and outside of the tell settlements, people and property may still have been the target of attacks.

Whatever the truth, when we move forward in time to the tells built c. 4500 BC and after in the later stages of the Final Neolithic in north-east Bulgaria, the situation appears to be rather different. At these sites, the multiple enclosures disappear and houses are instead enclosed inside more complex rectangular enclosures comprising substantial wattle-and-daub walls with multiple timber posts; some of these enclosures also feature baffle gates. Many of these settlements were destroyed by fires, which were revealed by the thick destruction layers of burnt material found at them. It seems that at least in some cases, these fires were sudden and unexpected, forcing people to abandon settlements and leave behind possessions and produce. For example, at the site of Ovcharovo large numbers of pottery vessels (some of which contained carbonised grain) and many grinding stones were left behind by its inhabitants. It is also interesting to note that at some sites such as Poljanitsa III, the fiercest areas of burning are found at the enclosure walls and entrances, hinting that these areas were deliberately targeted by enemy raiders.

Even more telling is the evidence recovered by archaeologists at Ruse on the lower Danube. At this important site the remains of some seventy people were found in burials scattered across the settlement mound, with some located between the burnt houses of the village (the normal burial practice was exhumation in separate cemeteries outside villages), and it is quite probable that many of these people died at the same time in a single catastrophic event. Both individual and multiple burials of up to six people were discovered with the latter burial tradition dominating the funerary record at Ruse. It is clear that in some cases, bodies were simply tossed carelessly into graves or pits, suggesting a lack of respect for the dead. For example, one grave contained an adult skeleton lying on its back with its arms outstretched. Lying on top of it was another adult skeleton in a crouched position, and four children were buried in the grave also. A hole in the skull of this adult revealed that he/she had been struck in the head with some sort of weapon, and sadly, we may be looking at the massacre of a single family with this particular grave.

The most compelling evidence, however, for the attack and destruction of a Bulgarian Late Neolithic tell has been uncovered at the superb site of Yunatsite in the Upper Thracian Valley, southern Bulgaria. Excavations carried out here by the noted Russian archaeologist Nicolai Merpert uncovered grisly evidence of its violent end. All of the houses in the settlement had been burned down, and lying on the floors or between the walls of the houses, were the remains of some fifty men, women, and children, very probably representing families in some cases. In one house, the skeletons of seven people were discovered, and the unnatural positions of several of the bodies (e.g. lying on the floor face down) suggested that no care had been taken in the burial of the dead. Many of the skulls also bore traces of violence, and thus taken as a whole, the evidence points towards a massacre in which many people died. On the basis of dates obtained from two skeletons found in recent excavations at the settlement, this appears to have taken place around 4200 BC, some 700 years after it was founded.

Recent excavations at Yunatsite have also recovered the remains of a deep ditch and substantial clay wall (measuring a very substantial 5 m in width) surrounding the 'uptown section' of the settlement. The possible remnants of a burnt, wooden gate-tower that had collapsed vertically have also been found, and also of interest is the intriguing female skeleton (the woman was aged c. 50–55 years – a very good age for the Neolithic) discovered by archaeologists working at Yunatsite in 2006. Remarkably, she appears to have survived the amputation of her right hand for some time – perhaps for several years – revealing considerable prehistoric surgical skills, and perhaps also the use of some form of narcotic plant as an anaesthetic. Although it is probably unlikely (but not impossible) that this woman lost her hand in warfare, her hasty burial in a rough grave between houses on the very edge of the settlement may indicate that she lost her life in the enemy assault that destroyed it. In light of the evidence from Yunatsite, the site of Kubrat should also be mentioned, as here too, archaeologists found human remains mixed in with the debris of houses that had been burnt to the ground. It seems likely that the people found in the houses were also killed as the result of an enemy attack on settlement.

The tell settlement of Provadia in north-eastern Bulgaria is also of some interest to us. Here, lying below a huge tell, which is capped by a later Thracian burial mound (the tell measures some 21 m in height and 30 m in diameter), archaeologists have discovered one of the oldest 'towns' in prehistoric Europe, dating from c. 5500–4200 BC. Numerous artefacts have been recovered from the site including fine decorated pots, a 'Mother Goddess' stone figurine, flint and bone arrowheads and spearheads, and copper objects (e.g. earrings and an axe). Strong evidence (e.g. ovens and deep pits in which brine was evaporated in ceramic vessels and huge tubs) indicating that Provadia was an important salt-production centre through-out its history, has also come to light during the excavations. This is hardly surprising given that the settlement is located on top of one of largest depos-its of salt in south-eastern Europe.

During the later stages of the settlements history (c. 4700–4200 BC), it was surrounded by a series of what appear to be a series of three suc-cessive fortification systems: a wooden-earthen palisade and two massive stone-walled enclosures. These stone walls feature bastions, measure 2–3 m thick and are least 3 m high in places, with large stone blocks weighing up to 5 tonnes. Bastions are a common feature of military fortifications and are external projections of a larger wall, which enable defenders of a site to inflict flanking fire on any approaching attackers.

A deep moat has also been discovered in front of the south-eastern gate at Provadia, and thus considering all of the site's architectural features as a whole, it is hard to escape the conclusion that the Neolithic people of Provadia took impressive measures to protect their settlement from potential attack. It is quite possible that the fortifications were erected to protect the wealth generated by the production of salt, which was one of the most valuable commodities of prehistoric (and later historic) Europe. Not all scholars may agree with this hypothesis, but it is certainly a plausible one worth consid ering. Archaeologists working at Provadia have also uncovered a cemetery in which some of the inhabitants of this remarkable Late Neolithic settlement were buried. One of the burials in this cemetery contained what appears to be the grave of a family, all of whom had died violently.

A Neolithic Massacre in Romania?

The substantial Neolithic settlement of Lumea Nouă (over 40 hectares in size) in Romania was discovered accidentally in 1942 during building work in the city of Alba Iulia (Transylvania). Since then, the settlement has been the subject of several successive archaeological campaigns, and during res-cue excavations carried out here from 2002–2008, a large quantity of human bones (dated to 4600–4450 BC) belonging to both adults and children were discovered in pits associated with a former dwelling. It was clear from the jumbled nature of these bones that not much care had been taken in the burial of the dead, with the remains of c. 100 individuals being simply thrown into the pits. Traces of an intense fire that must have destroyed the house were also identified in the pits and on the bones. It should also be noted that three enclosure ditches have been identified at the site, two of which have V-shaped sections.

In respect of the intriguing human remains found at Lumea Nouă, Mihai Gligor has said: 'The preliminary archaeological information suggested the fact that at a certain moment the local community [were] faced with an unusual number of people who died at the same time. This might have been caused by an epidemic or a massacre [that occurred during] a large conflict'.[12] At first, no evidence for an epidemic was noted on the bones, nor were there any obvious signs (i.e. embedded projectile points) that these people had died violently. However, a closer look at the skulls from the pits revealed 'bottomed fractures' in similar places, which were caused by powerful blows from a blunt object of some sort. The fact that the fractures were also of similar shape and dimensions indicated that the same weapon had been used to administer these blows, and the likelihood is that the weapon in question was a polished stone axe.

Many archaeologists have also argued that the perforated stone mace heads, and stone and copper shaft-hole axes, which were a feature of the Balkan Late Neolithic, were primarily designed with warfare in mind. Such axes are most famously found in the 'chieftain's' grave (Fig. 5) at the remarkable cemetery discovered at Varna on the Black Sea coast of Bulgaria, where many graves yielded a staggering amount of gold artefacts (over 3000), as well as numerous other fine objects. It is could be possible that the obviously important individual buried in this grave gained his elite status because of his prowess and bravery in warfare. Many graves in the Varna cemetery (some of which were 'cenotaph' graves that did not contain bodies) contained weapons such as the copper spear points found in Graves 97 and 43 that can only have been used to kill animals or humans (or both). Large caches of fired-clay balls have also been found at some settlements of the famous Vinča culture of the Neolithic Balkans, and like the Greek examples mentioned above, it is quite possible that they were sling-shots used in the defence of villages. Not all agree with this interpretation, with some arguing that these clay balls were temperature testers for baking, weights, or even toys. Whatever their true purpose, the evidence described briefly above surely reveals that for some Balkan Neolithic communities at least, warfare was a reality, and that some settlements came under attack from enemy raiding parties, with many people violently killed in these attacks.

Evidence from the Iron Gates Gorge

The Iron Gates Gorge of the Danube River, which forms part of the border between Romania and Serbia, is home to several important archaeological sites that have yielded abundant evidence pertaining to the Late Mesolithic/ Early Neolithic and the time of the transition from hunting and gathering to farming. The most famous site in the Gorge is Lepenski Vir, which is located on the banks of the Danube in eastern Serbia. This hugely important site was excavated during the 1960s and much remarkable evidence for a river-side settlement dating to the Late Mesolithic/Early Neolithic (c. 6300–5500 BC) was uncovered. This included the stone footings of somewhat peculiar, trapezoidal-shaped dwellings featuring large stone hearths. Even more peculiar were the numerous carved sandstone boulders found near these hearths, which depicted hybrid fish-human beings. Nobody can know for sure what these amazing prehistoric sculptures signify, but it may be that they represented the dead who had been transformed into aquatic supernatural beings. It could also be the case that they reveal a strong cultural identity, and are an expression of native resistance to incoming farming groups of the Balkan Neolithic Starčevo culture, who were settling in the Iron Gates region.

In fact, possible evidence for armed conflict between the Late Mesolithic natives of the Gorge and these groups, was found at Lepenski Vir and the contemporaneous site of Vlasac, which lies some 5 km downstream of the former. It has to be admitted, however, that this evidence is rather limited, and takes the form of a small, healed depressed fracture, and a blunt-force trauma (the possible cause of death) seen on a male skull from Vlasac, and a healed depressed fracture seen on a male skull from Lepenski Vir, that appears to have been produced by an object with a sharp and rounded end. It could perhaps be possible that the object in question was a Neolithic stone axe.

Much stronger evidence for warfare has been found at the hunter-gatherer site of Schela Cladovei, which is located in a fertile floodplain on the left bank of the Danube, over 100 km downstream from the above two sites. Of the twenty-eight individuals excavated at this site, seven had clearly been involved in violent conflict, and some had almost certainly died as a result. This evidence included a male and female skull displaying blunt-force trauma, one male and one female with parry fractures on their forearms, one man with a bone arrowhead embedded in his skull, and an individual of unknown sex with a flint arrowhead stuck in his/her bones. The radiocarbon dates obtained from these human remains suggest that these individuals may have been involved in armed conflict in the Late Mesolithic/Early Neolithic, when the first farmers were appearing in the Iron Gates region.

Chapter 2

Warfare in the *Linearbandkeramik /* Linear Pottery Culture

In the first half of the sixth millennium BC, a new and distinctive Neolithic culture known as the *Linearbandkeramik* (LBK) or Linear Pottery culture (c. 5700–4900 BC) emerged on the Hungarian plain, from where it quickly spread into central Europe and beyond: LBK sites are found not only in France, Belgium and the Netherlands but also Poland, the Ukraine and Moldovia. The origins of the LBK are not completely clear and continue to be a matter of debate amongst archaeologists. Archaeological evidence perhaps suggests that Late Mesolithic hunter-gatherer communities in the Lake Baláton area, who were in contact with neighbouring migrant Neolithic ones of the Balkan Starčevo culture, lie behind the emergence of the LBK, with the hunter-gatherers becoming 'Neolithisized' as a result of this contact. However, the swift expansion of the *Linearbandkeramik* across large parts of Europe, and its strong cultural identity, suggests that it represents a movement of colonising farmers. In light of this idea, it is interesting to note that studies of ancient DNA indicate that the ancestral roots of the *Linearbandkeramik* farmers lie in the Near East and Anatolia.

Whatever the truth is in respect of the origins of the LBK, its widespread communities have left us with fascinating traces of their prehistoric lives, such as the striking pottery featuring bands of incised decoration (Fig. 6), from which this culture take its name, or the remains of the substantial longhouses in which they (and their animals) lived. LBK longhouses were often large constructions and could even reach an impressive 70 m in length, and it is probable that some of the larger examples housed several families or functioned as community meeting places. It is also evident from the archaeological evidence found at some LBK sites, that undoubtedly, relations were not always amicable between the communities of this famous early farming culture. This has been most famously shown at the site of Talheim, the discovery of which played a large part in changing perceptions about a peaceful Neolithic Europe, revealing that sometimes, the people of Europe's first farming communities visited savage violence on each other.

The Talheim Massacre

In 1983, a man was digging in his garden at Talheim, southern Germany, and must have been more than a little perturbed when he came across human bones. Not surprisingly, he informed the local police, and after it had been ascertained that the bones were not modern in date, archaeologists were soon on the scene. They subsequently uncovered a trough-shaped pit containing a confused mass of human bones, representing the remains of at least thirty-four skeletons dating to the later LBK c. 4900 BC (Fig. 7). Scattered amongst the skeletal remains were numerous sherds from smashed LBK pottery vessels along with fragments of wattle and daub, suggesting that the pit had been cut into an earlier one used for the disposal of settlement refuse. Joachim Wahl and Iris Trautmann have remarked on the significance of this discovery: 'For the first time in research history, we encountered evidence that questioned the accepted stereotypical picture of the peaceful farmer and it is still viewed today as the earliest proof of warfare by some prehistorians worldwide'.[1]

It was clear from the orientation of the skeletons that the dead (who had perhaps been stripped of their clothes before burial) had simply been thrown into the pit at the same time. Later analysis of the bones revealed that they belonged to both children and adults of various ages, with the youngest child aged about two years old and the oldest adult around sixty years of age (a very good age given that few people in LBK communities lived past thirty years). In total, sixteen individuals were under twenty years of age, and eighteen were adults, probably representing most, if not all of the inhabitants of a small LBK farming village. However, the possibility that they were part of a larger population from a more substantial settlement cannot be totally ruled out. Either way, it was evident from a closer inspection of the skeletons that twenty skulls featured large, unhealed (and in some cases, multiple) fractures. Analysis of these fractures revealed that people had been clubbed to death by the stone axes and shoe last adzes typically used by LBK farmers. The location of the skull wounds and their angle of impact, indicates that their attackers had been located behind their victims, who had been trying to escape. Three individuals also show signs of having been shot from behind by arrowheads, which suggests that this attack had taken place during the daytime.

The fact that only some of the skeletons displayed lethal wounds should not be taken as evidence that not all of the people in the pit had met a violent end, as we must take into account the strong possibility that they died as a result of lethal wounds to soft tissue, which have left no traces on bones. The grim evidence discovered at Talheim thus points strongly towards a surprise attack on a LBK hamlet or village and the subsequent massacre of most, if not all of its inhabitants, by a rival LBK community, with the dead casually dumped into a make-shift grave.

The Talheim massacre has been likened to another well-known prehistoric massacre that was discovered at Crow Creek in South Dakota, although the archaeological evidence uncovered at this site goes way beyond that from the Talheim death-pit in terms of the numbers of people killed. This village of the native Coalescent tradition was built around 1325 AD on a steep-ridge above the Missouri River floodplain, and was first excavated during the 1950s, with the remains of at least fifty houses and two fortification ditches unearthed (the inner ditch was 20 ft wide by 6 ft deep, while the outer was 12 ft wide by 6 ft deep). The first signs of this massacre came to light in 1978, when human remains were spotted eroding out of one of the fortification ditches. A salvage excavation to recover this material subsequently revealed a 'bone bed' comprising the skeletons of around 490 people (with an estimated c. 50 unexcavated skeletons remaining in place in the ditch), most of which bore evidence for extreme violence and lethal assault. For example, c. 40 per cent of the skulls had one or more depressed fractures caused by blows to the head, with some skulls displaying up to five fractures, and around 90 per cent of the skulls bore cut-marks that were indicative of scalping. The scalping victims ranged in age from less than a year to sixty years old. Other cut marks seen on the skeletons point to the slitting of noses and the removal of tongues from holes slit in the throats of the dead (or the living?). Many skeletons also have missing skulls, hands, and feet, indicating trophy taking by those responsible for this shocking event. The bone-bed discovered at Crow Creek must surely represent the slaughter of an entire Coalescent community by an enemy force, or most of the members of this village, as young women were under-represented in the skeletal assemblage, perhaps indicating that they were taken as slaves. It could be possible that the Crow Creek community was attacked by another Coalescent group or groups, who were competing for scarce farming land and resources, in an overpopulated region with an unstable climate.

In fact, archaeological evidence pertaining to prehistoric massacres in America is not that uncommon, and another important site in this regard is the south-western Sacred Ridge Site, Colorado. Here twenty-two pit dwellings dating to the early Pueblo I period (c. 700–900 AD) were excavated, with several collections of human bone bearing signs of violence found on the floors of the houses by the American archaeologists. The most notable of these was found in Feature 104 with the bone assemblage consisting of a minimum number of thirty-five individuals of all ages and both sexes. James Potter and Jason Chuipka have documented the harrowing nature of these human remains:

> ....in each case, the systematic destruction of the entire body was evident from head to toe...foot bones were broken and the bottoms of feet, cut, chopped, and scraped. Several individuals had under-gone removal of the scalp, nose and/or ears...other common dam-age to the skull and face included the smashing of the front teeth, the disarticulation of the lower jaw, and blunt force trauma on, and subsequent breakage and burning of, the cranium. [2]

Potter and Chuipka have suggested that the savage massacre which had clearly occurred at Sacred Heart Ridge could be related to a combination of factors: a deteriorating climate (colder and drier), overhunting of local game, limited land for growing crops, and a growing population, with Pueblo I communities in this area turning violently against each other as a result. Whatever the case, there can be little doubt that the community that once lived at Sacred Heart Ridge was wiped out by a rival group who showed no quarter.

The Asparn/Schletz and Schöneck-Killianstädten Massacres

The site of Talheim does not stand alone as a beacon of brutality in the central European LBK, as mass graves containing massacred individuals have also been found at the sites of Asparn/Schletz, Lower Austria, and Schöneck-Killianstädten near Frankfurt. Turning to the former site first, archaeological investigations have been ongoing here since its discovery in 1983, and a large settlement enclosed by two substantial ditches (c. 4 m wide and 2 m deep) featuring probable gateways has been uncovered. Numerous artefacts (e.g. pottery, bone and stone tools), were recovered from the enclo-sure ditches and at the base of the outer one, the mostly incomplete skeletons of sixty-seven people were also discovered. Radiocarbon dates indicate that the settlement was occupied in the middle/later LBK 5210–4950 BC. It has been noted in regard to these skeletons that, 'They were found in atypical postures, often in prone positions with randomly crossed limbs and unnatu-rally bent torsos',[3] revealing that the dead had been haphazardly tossed into the ditch. The dead included both adults and children (four babies were also identified among the children) and it was clear from their injuries that they had not met a peaceful end. The lethal fractures seen on the skulls showed that all but one individual (a teenager who had been shot in the head with an arrow) had been clubbed to death with LBK axes and adzes, and that powerful blows had been directed both to the back of people's skulls and their faces. Interestingly, young women were under-represented amongst the dead, which may indicate that they were abducted by the enemy group who attacked the settlement.

The dead would have been in something of a state when they were thrown into the ditch, as there were animal gnaw marks on the bones (and many also had their hands and feet missing), indicating that the bodies were left lying out in the open for some time before burial. It is also interesting to note that only around 20 per cent of the ditch at Asparn/Schletz has so far been excavated, which raises the question of how many other 'war dead' may actually lie here waiting to be discovered? In fact, it is quite possible that the whole of the outer ditch is filled with the skeletons of people who died in an enemy attack. If so, then several hundred people representing most of the population of the Asparn/Schletz LBK settlement may have been massacred in a fierce enemy assault.

Like Talheim, the Schöneck-Killianstädten mass grave was found by chance and only came to light as result of road building operations in 2006, when construction workers hit upon jumbled up human remains lying at the base of a long V-shaped pit. This pit may well have been part of a larger ditch enclosing the substantial LBK settlement that was also found during the construction of the road (the remains of some eighteen longhouses were identified). Scientific analysis of the bones revealed the remains of around twenty-six people, with both children and adults dumped into the pit (dating of the bones revealed that this took place in the later LBK between 5207–4849 BC). Ten of the children were less than six years old, with the youngest being aged no more than six months.

Numerous pertimortem fractures similar to those seen at Asparn/Schletz and Talheim were identified on skulls (again, likely to have been caused by stone axes and adzes) and it was also evident that many individuals had also received vicious blows to their arms and legs, as shown by the numerous perimortem fractures present on both arm and leg bones. Intriguingly, the highest number of fractures (over 50 per cent) were identified on the tibiae and fibulae (lower leg bones) of individuals, which could indicate that people were tortured before death by being smashed in the legs. Alternatively, it could perhaps be possible that their assailants meted out these blows in order to stop the vengeful ghosts of the dead pursuing them. [4] Whatever the motivation for this violent practice, the evidence from Schöneck-Killianstädten further weakens the argument that warfare was of little significance in Neolithic Europe. Two bone arrowheads, which had probably originally been lodged in bodies, were also found when the soil adhering to the Schöneck-Killianstädten skeletal material was removed in the laboratory, and two lesions that may be attributable to arrowhead injuries were also noted on two vertebrae. Furthermore, at least one humerus (upper arm bone) showed clear chop marks, indicating amputation.

As is the case at Asparn/Schletz, it appears that some people escaped the killing at Schöneck-Killianstädten, as only a few younger women and teenagers were found among the dead. In regard to the former, it could be possible that as at Asparn/Schletz, these women were taken captive by those responsible for the massacre and forcibly integrated into an enemy community (where it is perhaps possible they became slaves). The teenagers may also have suffered the same fate, or perhaps they escaped because they were fitter and fleeter of foot, also having no children to protect like older members of the community. If young women and teenagers were indeed forced into captivity as a result of the LBK massacres discussed here, it is sobering to think that several of them would surely have lost family members and friends in the attacks carried out on their villages. Indeed, scientific analysis of the skeletons from Talheim has identified two possible brothers, and a father and his two children, providing us with a sad reminder that the mutilated bones found at this site once belonged to people who probably had to witness their loved ones dying a horrific death.

Herxheim

The highly intriguing evidence found at the site of Herxheim, south-western Germany, may also provide us with further proof of an LBK massacre, although it has to be admitted that in this respect, it is more ambiguous than that found at the above three sites. During the two archaeological campaigns that were undertaken here between 1996–1999 and 2005–2008, numerous human bones were found in the two trapezoidal ditches surrounding this later LBK settlement that was inhabited between 5300 and 4950 BC. Bruno Boulestin et al. have argued that these ditches (which reached up to 4 m deep in some places) could never have served a defensive purpose, as they are 'pseudo-ditches' formed from a series of overlapping oblong pits of various dimensions, 'which were dug over several centuries according to a pre-determined layout'.[5] The remains of some five hundred individuals were found in these 'pseudo-ditches', and, given that they have not been fully excavated (around 50 per cent of the ditches remain unexcavated), the remains of many more people are suspected, with perhaps as many as 1000 people originally buried in them.

Undoubtedly, the most curious (and rather extraordinary) aspect of the skeletal evidence from Herxheim are the c. 500 calottes or bone 'skull caps' found in the ditches, which in some cases, were carefully stacked on top of each other in 'nests'. It is evident from analysis of these calottes that they were all removed from skulls using the same procedures, with well-aimed blows to the frontal bones (mainly to the centre of foreheads) removing the other facial bones; systematic blows were aimed at the skulls resulting in evenly shaped calottes being produced.

Of course this rather bizarre (at least to our eyes) practice does not provide proof of a massacre/warfare, and it may well be the case that the calottes point to the complex treatment of human bones in a peaceful ritual, the understanding of which lies beyond our reach. However, this argument is perhaps weakened by the fact that the skeletons from Herxheim were buried without the proper or normal care usually reserved for the LBK dead, and furthermore, the existence of armed conflicts at the site is revealed by healed injuries on some of the skulls. One such skull displayed four healed injuries that had been received in at least two violent encounters, with the most severe injury probably caused by the blade of an LBK stone adze, or axe. Although the individual who received this to the head, appears to have survived his injury for quite some time (which was actually not completely healed at the time of death), it is likely to have led to long lasting neurological defects such as a loss of speech or the inability to recognise and name people and objects. It also may be interesting to note that several ancient cultures are reported to have made calottes from the skulls of their enemies (e.g. the Scythians and the ancient Chinese) and to have used them as eating or drinking vessels. Several archaeologists are also of the opinion that the skull caps found at the well-known Late Palaeolithic site of Gough's Cave (c.13, 000 BC) in Somerset (where strong evidence for cannibalism was also found) were actually used as skull 'cups'.

Along with the strange skull caps found at Herxheim, possible but disputed evidence for cannibalism was also found at the site. In fact, Boulestin and his colleagues have argued that this evidence strongly indicates 'that the site was dedicated to ritual activities in which cannibalism played an important part'.[6] This evidence was uncovered from the lower levels of one of the ditches ('deposit 9') during the excavations that took place at Herxheim during the summer of 2007 and consists of the remains of at least ten people including both children and adults. The bones of these people display cut marks, which reveal that their corpses had first been cut up and butchered in a similar way to animals, and that their heads were also skinned and their tongues removed. This evidence, then, seems to suggest that at least some of the people who ended up in the ditches at Herxheim were being cannibalised and used for food. Whether it was survival or funerary/ritual cannibalism ['endocannibalism'] or war cannibalism [aggressive 'exocannibalism'] is open to question, but given the other skeletal evidence from Herxheim, perhaps the latter is more likely.

Other LBK sites in Germany have yielded further possible evidence of cannibalism such as the Jungfernhöhle ('virgin's/maids cave') in Upper Franconia, Bavaria. Located in a beautiful forest and associated with folk tales about women who been killed and eaten, this small but atmospheric cave was scientifically excavated after two local treasure hunters unearthed pottery and human bones here in 1951. As well as late LBK pottery (some 110 vessels) Dr Otto Kunkel and his team found the bones of around forty people (at least 23 children or adolescents, 1 or 2 men, and c. 11 women), which have been radiocarbon dated to about 5100 BC. Some of the long bones may have been smashed for their marrow, and teeth were also missing from many skulls, perhaps suggesting that they were war trophies taken to be worn as amulets or jewellery. It is interesting to note that a necklace made from human teeth was also found at a similarly dated LBK burial ground in Nitra, Slovakia. It should be mentioned that after a re-examination of the bones from the Jungfernhöhle, it has been argued that they have no connection with violence, and rather, they were brought to the cave from bodies that had decayed elsewhere, to receive secondary burial along with pottery and animal bones. It seems unlikely that we will ever know the truth, but the lack of men in the skeletal sample is curious. Could it be possible the evidence from the Jungfernhöhle represents the remnants of an LBK community who had escaped from a violent attack on their settlement, later being caught hiding fearfully in the cave by those responsible for this attack? A speculative idea undoubtedly, but one perhaps worth considering, nonetheless.

There are in fact, numerous ethnographic accounts of warfare cannibalism, which was often carried out in order to terrify and humiliate enemies, and also because it was believed that the living would absorb the vital energies or souls of the dead, as a result, becoming more powerful and courageous warriors. One example is provided by the Wari' people of southern Amazonia, who until the 1960s, ate the flesh of their enemies. They carried the body parts of their dead enemies – heads, arms and legs – in baskets, back to their villages (just as they did with hunted animals), where they were roasted. Alternatively, if the walk back from the enemy settlement they had attacked was too lengthy, the body parts would be roasted in the forest.

Strong evidence for warfare cannibalism has also been found at several Native American sites, such as Polacca Wash in Arizona, where around thirty massacred Hopi villagers of all ages were found in a burial pit (most of the dead were probably females). This mass burial was excavated in 1964 by Alan P. Olson and his colleagues. However, the fragmented bones recovered from the site, which had been stored at the Museum of Northern Arizona, were largely forgotten, until anthropologist Christy Turner stumbled across them while carrying out other research at the museum. Her subsequent analysis of the bones uncovered not only evidence of shocking violence but also strong indications of cannibalism. The condition of the people's skulls revealed that all of them had been clubbed in the head, with many receiving shattering blows to their faces, with all but one skull displaying 20–25 injuries, indicating a frenzied assault that probably also involved the decapitation of some individuals. All of the skulls also had the brain exposed, which Christy Turner and Nancy Morris plausibly argued provides strong evidence of cannibalism. Further skeletal evidence to support this claim was seen on the long bones, which displayed cut-marks and breakage patterns, strongly suggesting that they had been intentionally broken in order to expose the marrow within.[7]

It is also interesting to note that the Polacca Wash site is known in Hopi legend as the 'Ghost/Death Mound', and is said to be the burial place of people from the large mesa top village of Awatobi, who were captured in a raid carried out in 1700 AD, by an alliance of Hopi warriors from five nearby villages. According to the legend, as the captives (who were mainly young women and children) were being taken back to their captor's villages, many were killed, mutilated, and dismembered. It seems that the raid was carried out on the inhabitants of Awatobi in retaliation for their collusion with Spanish Christian missionaries and the resulting witchcraft that they were allegedly practicing on other Hopi Villages.

Further examples of warfare cannibalism include those recorded in southern Central America, with a Colombian chief and his followers are reputed to have eaten – in a single day – the bodies of one hundred enemies defeated in battle. On the island of Fiji, one chief is documented as keeping a tally of all the enemies he had eaten, by placing a stone representing each victim behind his house; 872 stones stretched in a line measuring nearly 200 m.

In fact, it may perhaps be the case, that warfare cannibalism has a very ancient pedigree reaching far back into the human story. At the important Lower Palaeolithic cave-site of Gran Dolina, in the Sierra de Atapuerca region of central Spain, one of the numerous archaeological levels (TD6) excavated within its confines yielded the skeletal remains of at least eleven early humans or 'hominins' (classified as the species *Homo antecessor*). The individuals were of varying ages, although eight of them were under fourteen years of age. Their bones were found randomly mixed together with many wild animal ones and stone tools. Dating to around 800,000 years ago, this level has been interpreted as representing the remains of a *Homo antecessor* camp site, where both hunted animals and humans were butchered and eaten. This hypothesis is supported by the fact that both sets of bones display similar cut marks and breakage patterns, which relate to the butchery of both animal and human carcasses. The apparent cannibalism at TD6 could have been part of a subsistence strategy by *H. antecessor* against another group who were competing for resources and territory, and perhaps provides us with the earliest evidence for warfare.

While I was writing this book, further possible evidence of similar behaviour to that witnessed at TD6 broke in the popular press, with the media reporting an important discovery made at the Goyet caves near Namur, Belgium. Neanderthal bones dating to c. 40–45,000 years ago were recovered from the cave, along with numerous horse and reindeer bones, both of which bore cut marks relating to butchery and marrow extraction. Some of the Neanderthal bones found in the cave, which came from four adults or teenagers, and a child, also appear to have been used as flint-knapping tools. If this evidence does reveal Neanderthal cannibalism, it does not prove that an act of warfare cannibalism was practiced by another Neanderthal group (or possibly, an incoming modern human one – although there is no evidence for *Homo sapiens* in Belgium at this time). However, starvation cannibalism seems improbable, as the Neanderthal bones were found jumbled together with wild animal ones. Thus these ancient bones more probably represent either endocannibalism or exocannibalism.

Other skeletal pointing strongly towards warfare in the later LBK can also be mentioned, such as that found at Vaihingen (c. 5300–5100 BC) in the Neckar Valley (south-western Germany). Here, a dozen individuals were dumped in two large rubbish pits, with further scattered remains found throughout the site, contrasting with the typical burials dug into the ditch at a later date. The bones of these individuals bore various injuries and there were also signs of the mutilation of bodies. Some of the formal LBK burials in the ditch also bore signs of violence, with one individual, for example, apparently having been killed by a powerful blow to the skull. Interestingly, analysis of the bones found in the rubbish pits showed differences to those found in the ditches and it may be that they represent the remains of native, Late Mesolithic hunter-gatherers, who were killed by incoming LBK groups. The question of warfare between hunter-gatherer and LBK communities will be returned to below.

Moving westwards, there is the recent discovery made at the Mulhouse-Est LBK cemetery (dating to c. 5100 BC), which is lies just over the German border in Alsace, north-eastern France. Following the original excavations carried out at the site between 1964–1972, further ones were undertaken here in 2014, and two new burials were discovered. The first was very fragmentary and contained few grave goods (an iron ore nodule and a fragment from a *Spondylus* ornament). However, the other contained the very well-preserved skeleton of a young male (15–20 years of age who had been buried with a fire-lighting kit (a flint striker and piece of iron ore), a decorated pot, a *Spondylus* ring, an adze blade, and a rather unusual perforated antler axe. He had evidently died a violent death, as an arrowhead had been fired into his body just below his right clavicle, lodging between his top two ribs on the right side. The young man may not have died immediately after he was shot by the arrow, but the lack of evidence for any healing strongly suggests that he lost his life soon after this violent event.

A Crisis in the LBK?

Whatever motivated warfare in the latter half of the LBK can obviously never be known for sure, but the archaeological evidence discussed above clearly shows that its early Neolithic farming communities engaged in brutal and exterminative warfare. However, it may be that adverse climatic conditions (fluctuating periods of heavy rainfall and prolonged dry periods) c. 5500 BC, coupled with an expanding population, led to an escalation in warfare during this time. As Meyer et al. have stated: 'As previous research has shown, climatic changes, especially those leading to increasing unpredictability of or even significant decreases in agricultural production, have played major roles in the change and collapse of societies throughout human history'.[8] They have also suggested that as well as ecological imbalance leading to perceived or actual resource stress, in the later LBK, warfare in general might have been further aggravated by unequal social access to good quality farmland, food, and perhaps also prestige goods.[9] It could also be the case that some warfare in the LBK was motivated by a desire to avenge the taking of women by enemy raiders, as suggested by Wahl and Trautmann in respect of the cause of the Talheim massacre. Some support for this idea may be provided by the discovery of LBK pottery sherds in the upper levels of the Talheim death pit, which feature decoration that is more characteristic of LBK pots made many miles away in the Stuttgart region.[10] Of course, this interesting but specualtive theory not only assumes that LBK women made pots and not men, and does not consider that foreign pottery could have reached the Talheim area through trade and exchange. Nonetheless, it is possible that in some cases at least, LBK warfare was motivated by a desire to mete out violent retribution – and to recapture – women, men, or children, who had been taken in successful raids on enemy settlements.

It may be that the evident increase in warfare in the later LBK, which seems to have brought LBK culture to a swift demise, was connected to a severe geological event in the region of the Black Sea shelf at this time. As a result of this event, which flooded 100,000 km² of agricultural land, there may have been gradual waves of migration into central Europe, which would have naturally led to a rise in population levels. This rise in population may have brought about conflicts over farming resources and land, although somewhat curiously it seems that warfare was much more intense in the western part of the LBK distribution than in the eastern one. This raises the possibility that other driving forces rather than climate change account for the warfare that obviously erupted here some seven thousand years ago, although future archaeological discoveries in the eastern LBK distribution may redress this imbalance.

LBK Enclosures

Several archaeologists are of the opinion that the enclosure ditches surrounding later (and earlier) LBK sites were mainly defensive features, which in some cases (e.g. Asparn/Schletz), tragically failed to serve their purpose. Many other LBK ditched enclosures are known, some of which also feature palisades, and there are also sites that are surrounded by just palisades. Not all agree, however, that LBK enclosures were defensive in nature, and for example, it has been argued that 'They may have served to reinforce...a sense of purely local identity and independence, either by providing an arena for gatherings or simply by symbolically capturing spaces with a long tradition of communal activity'.[11] Admittedly, it seems very improbable that all LBK enclosures represent fortifications and were indeed used as gathering places for religious and secular activities, and some were probably used for penning and controlling livestock. However, given the grim evidence described above, it would be hardly surprising that at least some LBK communities would wish to defend themselves from the possible threat of attack (real or imagined) by building fortifications around some of their sites.

Mark Golitiko and Lawrence Keeley have undertaken a review of LBK ditched enclosures[12] and interestingly, they have found that over 60 per cent of these sites are found in the western part of the LBK distribution, which as noted above, appears to have been more warlike in nature than the eastern one. Furthermore, Golitko and Keeley have also discovered that c.60 per cent of all known LBK enclosures feature V- or Y- shaped ditches that average c. 3 m wide by 1.5 m deep. As mentioned in the previous chapter, V- or Y-shaped ditches are a classic defensive feature of both ancient and more recent fortified sites around the world. As Golitko and Keeley also point out in respect of the LBK ditches, they have typically eroded over time by 0.5–1 m, and therefore, many of them would originally been 'easily as deep or deeper than the height of any potential early Neolithic attacker'. Furthermore, they have argued that 70 per cent of LBK sites possess features (i.e. complex gate arrangements, palisades and ditches) that can be interpreted as defensive features, also rightly noting that there is a 'distinct association between enclosed sites' and the skeletal evidence revealing the existence of LBK warfare.

Darion, Oleye and Longchamps: Evidence of Frontier Warfare in the LBK?

Excavations carried out from 1984–1991 by the Institut Royal de Sciences Naturelles de Belgique and the University of Illinois, at the three Late LBK settlements of Darion, Oleye and Longchamps in the Hesbaye region of north-east Belgium did not yield any LBK war casualties. However, they did bring to light archaeological evidence which strongly suggested that these sites were fortified against attack. In contrast to that found at the above LBK settlements, however, this evidence probably indicates that the people living in these early farming villages on the western limits or 'frontier' of LBK expansion, wished to protect themselves from potentially hostile groups of native late hunter-gatherers, rather than neighbouring LBK ones. These three sites form part of an LBK settlement 'cluster' or 'cell' containing several villages that was located along the Upper reaches of the River Geer. It is certainly of some interest that this LBK cell is separated from contemporaneous Late Mesolithic sites to the north, by an empty zone some 25–30 km wide, where no significant geographical barrier exists. The existence of this 'no-man's-land' suggests that relations between LBK 'pioneers' (who appear to have arrived from the Dutch Limburg region c. 5250 BC) and the native hunter-gatherers in the Hesbaye were not particularly cordial. In fact, there are hints that that two of these settlements may actually have been attacked by Mesolithic raiding parties, although admittedly, the evidence for this scenario is far from unequivocal.

Turning first to Darion, the excavations here uncovered the ground plans of four LBK longhouses, the largest of which (c. 32 m in length) may have perhaps been deliberately burnt down. The most notable aspect of the site however, is the deep V-shaped ditch (over 2 m deep originally) that surrounds the settlement area, which covers an area measuring some 1.6 hectares. The ditch was originally backed by an internal palisade, and the remains of a complex arrangement of palisades at the southern end of the enclosure suggests the former existence of a baffle gate. There was also a double line of palisades at the enclosure's northern end, and a rectangular arrangement of post holes also found here was interpreted as a possible 'battlement or tower foundation'. It could perhaps even be possible that the latter resembled the fighting stages that the Maori built to strengthen the defences of their fortified $p\bar{a}$ settlements. Whatever the truth, the ditch and the remains of the associated architectural features at Darion, are certainly suggestive of the former existence of a fortified enclosure.

At Oleye, which was a much larger settlement covering some 6 hectares, the remains of eight longhouses were recovered, and these were surrounded by a very similar 'defensive' enclosure to that at Darion, which consisted of a V-profiled ditch (over 2 m deep) and internal palisade. A magnetometer survey of the site's interior also suggested that a baffled gate had been located at the northern end of the enclosure. Five of the longhouses had burnt down and this appears to have happened before the enclosure was built. It is quite possible that these burned houses may have been set ablaze by an enemy raiding party, although it could perhaps also be possible that they burnt down accidentally. Along with pottery and evidence for flint-working, a limited number of Mesolithic projectile points were found in the interior pits at Darion and Oleye. However, how they arrived on the two sites is far from clear, and it can only be tenuously suggested that they provide further evidence of Mesolithic raiding parties.

No burned houses or Mesolithic projectiles were found during the excavations at Longchamps, but as at Darion and Oleye, a V-shaped ditch over 2 m deep, which was backed by a palisade, was found on the eastern side of the enclosure. A complex arrangement of palisades that had probably formed a baffle gate, was also identified during the excavations undertaken at the site, and as at Darion a watch tower may have guarded the enclosure. Excavations carried out at other LBK villages in the Upper Geer region have also yielded further possible evidence for fortification. For example, at the site of Remicourt, archaeologists uncovered an enclosure ditch that was an impressive c.3.5 m deep, and a small section of palisade was also found. At the site of Fexhe le haut Clocher, there was a Y-sectioned ditch measuring 2.5 m in depth, and it is probable that there was also an internal palisade here too.

The LBK settlements briefly considered here, may not have ever been attacked by Mesolithic raiding parties, but if they were, the fact that bones do not survive well in the soil of the Hesbaye region, means that we are unlikely to find the remains of people killed in these attacks. Nevertheless, the evidence described briefly above arguably reveals that they were at least threatened by the possibility of such attacks, as Neolithic communities in other parts of Europe may well have been. Indeed, we might wonder whether the indigenous Mesolithic communities of Europe were all willing to peacefully accommodate the incoming Neolithic farming groups, who as in the Hesbaye, were establishing themselves in territories that long been held by hunter-gatherer communities. With this in mind, Katherine Spielmann and James Eder have argued that incoming Neolithic populations would of probably required a great of land for both planting their crops and for grazing their livestock, which would have put farmers and hunter-gatherers in potentially violent completion with one another.[13]

In fact, the first Neolithic fortifications to be erected as a defence against hunter-gatherers may have been built at the famous site of Jericho in Palestine. Around 8300 BC, the early Neolithic inhabitants (people of the Pre-Pottery Neolithic A or PPNA culture) of this substantial settlement erected a huge, freestanding stone wall around their site, which was 600 m long, some 4–5 m tall, and 1–2 m wide. A deep moat or ditch was also dug in front of the wall, and a stone tower measuring over 8 m high was also built behind the moat and wall. Not all scholars agree that the wall, ditch, and tower were defensive in nature, and it has been argued that the ditch and tower were flood defences and that the tower was a ritual building. However, it has been argued that, 'an acute threat from marauding hunter-gatherer groups to their stored crops, lives, and, indeed, uniquely fertile land would seem to have been the main factor that propelled the inhabitants of this pristine agricultural oasis to cluster together and undertake the labor involved in the massive defensive construction'.[14]

There are also many examples of hunter-gatherer raids on farmers to be found in the ethnographic record, and often, the prime objective of these raids were the domesticated animals owned by farming communities. Harvested produce was also sometimes targeted, although this would have been less easily obtainable than livestock, which was often located in fields or enclosures outside settlements. One such example comes from south-western America, with the defended settlements of the Pueblo agriculturalists who lived here, raided by bands of Apache and Navaho hunter-gatherers from the southern Great Plains. Sometimes, large Apache large war parties would also return to wreak vengeance on the inhabitants of settlements where warriors had been killed during raids. In southern Africa, the San Bushmen sometimes carried out cattle raids on their Bantu and Khoikhoi neighbours. These raids could also occasionally spiral out of control into open warfare. Of course, such anthropological evidence does not prove that similar raids occurred during the Mesolithic/Neolithic transition in Europe, with the vulnerable settlements of the Early Neolithic farmers targeted by native hunter-gatherer groups. However, it seems hard to believe that such raids never occurred at all.

Evidence from Post-LBK Cultures

Some sites of one of the LBK's 'daughter cultures', the Lengyel Culture (c. 5000–3400 BC), which developed out of the LBK in the Middle Danube region and then spread westwards and northwards, also display possible evidence for the existence of warfare. For example, there are the two well-known Polish Lengyel settlements of Brzéć Kujawski and Oslonki, where the ground plans of some eighty longhouses (not all contemporary) were discovered along with many artefacts. Both settlements also seem to have been located in parts of the landscape that would offer protection from raiding parties. Brzéć Kujawski is located on moraine, which forms a peninsula that juts out into a now largely dried-up lake, and would originally have been surrounded by water on three sides, while Oslonki is also surrounded on three sides by watery 'defences' in the form of marshland. Oslonki was also surrounded by a ditch and palisade, with a substantial timber gate. At both sites, there were houses that had burnt down, perhaps being deliberately set on fire by enemy raiders. It could be tentatively suggested that the individual – who to judge from the position of the skeleton – seems to have been carelessly dumped in one of the grain storage pits at Brzéć Kujawski, was a raider who been killed during an attack on the site.

Also of undoubted interest, is an intriguing burial that was found at Oslonki during the excavations carried out at here in the early 1990s. The male skeleton found in this burial displayed strong evidence for violent trauma in the form of severe fractures on his shins caused by a heavy implement of some sort and a large, and a presumably lethal fracture could also be seen on his skull. The skull was also found displaced from the rest of the skeleton in the grave, and the lack of most of the cervical vertebrae points towards the decapitation of this individual. Over twenty shallow cut-marks were also found on the man's skull near to where his left ear would have been, and these may indicate that one of his ears had been cut off with a flint knife or blade, and taken as a war trophy. The circumstances behind this individual's seemingly violent end are obviously open to interpretation, but it could be possible that he was an enemy captive who was tortured before being killed. However the fact that he was buried carefully and also with grave goods, seems to argue against this. Thus the alternative scenario is that he was a member of the Oslonki community who had received similar treatment at the hands of his enemies, but who had been laid to rest by his family and friends.

Rondels: Post-LBK Fortifications?

One of the characteristic features of the Lengyel, and other cultures that developed out of the Linearbandkeramik (e.g. the Stichbandkeramik/SBK) are the circular enclosures that are often referred to as 'rondels'. These sites are rather uniform in nature and comprise single or multiple circuits of ditch that are pierced by two or more entrances, which are often orientated on the cardinal points. Today, the traditional archaeological interpretation of these sites as Neolithic 'fortresses' or fortified settlements is seen as flawed, and many scholars have turned away from this idea, and now view them as ritual and ceremonial centres, connected with solar worship. However, even though such ideas find support in the general scarcity of evidence for domestic dwellings and activity inside many of these enclosures, this does not mean that some at least, doubled up as fortified sites for the Neolithic communities who constructed them.

For example, at the Lengyel culture site of Svodin in Slovakia, there were two impressive ditches and three palisades, with the ditches measuring

c. 5 m deep and between 4–8 m wide, which would have provided any attacking enemy force with a considerable obstacle. Although no evidence for domestic buildings was found inside the site, traces of probable houses were found on its perimeter along with an extensive cemetery (161 graves were excavated). Another possible fortified rondel of the Lengyel culture in Slovakia, is the site of Bučany, where postholes from a possible house were uncovered inside the palisade, which ran around the inner side of the two large ditches that enclosed the site. It has been reasonably suggested, that these and other Lengyel rondels in Slovakia, may have acted as ritual centres for the communities who built them, but they could also have acted as fortified refuges in times of danger.[15]

One of the most well-known Neolithic rondels is the one found at the important settlement of Bylany which is located near the town of Kutná Hora in the Czech Republic. Excavations carried out here in the latter half of the twentieth century revealed that a large settlement (c. 22 hectares in size) was established by people of the LBK (with many LBK longhouse plans and artefacts coming to light), and that successive phases of inhabitation had followed in the Lengyel and SBK periods.

The rondel was built by people of the Stichbandkeramik culture, and although no firm traces of SBK houses were found within its interior, there were the remains of an earlier LBK longhouse, LBK and SBK storage pits, three ovens, and over 100 postholes perhaps belonging to buildings of some sort. The rondel was found to consist of two ditches 115 m and 90 m in diameter, with four entrances. A further third ditch lying some 75 m away from this main enclosure, was also identified during at geophysical survey at the site. The inner ditch is 3 m wide and c. 2.5 m deep, while the outer ditch is of slightly smaller dimensions, measuring 2.5 m in width and just over 2 m deep. Both ditches have V-shaped profiles, which perhaps more than suggests that defence was on the mind of the people who dug them. Defensive concerns may also be revealed by the outer ditch entrances, which take the form of narrow corridors (8 m in length) that are formed by the curving ends of the outer ditches. Some artefacts were discovered in the bases of the ditches, among them Late SBK pottery sherds, grinding stones, daub, and animal bones. The slots from a complex system of three, if not four palisades, were also discovered inside the inner enclosure, and these may also have had a defensive function.

The idea that some Lengyel and SBK rondels functioned as 'forts' may be open to question, but evidence such as that found at the previously mentioned sites of Brześć Kujawski and Oslonki, suggests that whatever the true purpose of these enigmatic monuments, warfare was not unknown amongst the communities of these post-LBK cultures. In fact, it would arguably be a little strange if warfare was unknown in the Lengyel and SBK cultures. These two cultures led very similar lives to their LBK predecessors, and all the social and economic factors that would have fuelled LBK warfare, would have been present in these early farming societies also.

Chapter 3

Corded Ware and Bell Beaker Burials:
Evidence of Warfare *and* Warrior Groups?

The Corded Ware and Bell Beaker/Beaker Cultures represent two of the most famous archaeological phenomena of prehistoric Europe, and, on the basis of their widespread geographical spread, have rightly been termed 'supra-regional expansionist cultures'.[1] These hugely influential cultures, which both emerged c. 2900 BC, and subsequently spread into much of Europe, are named after the striking pottery that is often found accompanying the dead in their burials.

Traditionally, the origin of the Corded Ware Culture is seen to lie in north-central Europe, but a recent DNA study strongly suggests that instead, we should be looking to the vast region (the Pontic-Caspian Steppe) which stretches from the northern shores of the Black Sea in Romania to the Ural Mountains of Russia. This study compared DNA taken from nine skeletons of the Yamna/Yamnaya Culture, who lived in this extensive area, with that of four Corded Ware skeletons from Central Europe. As has been noted, the comparison of the two different sets of DNA 'showed that the four Corded Ware people could trace an astonishing three-quarters of their ancestry to the Yamnaya'.[2] Several scholars have also argued that the Yamnaya people spoke an early form of the Indo-European language and were responsible for its introduction and subsequent spread throughout Europe, with Marija Gimbutas the most notable of these (Gimbutas proposed that the Yamnaya were one of several groups who collectively comprised the larger 'Kurgan Culture'). In respect of Beaker Culture beginnings, archaeologists have proposed three separate homelands: Central Europe, the Netherlands, and Iberia. However, current research indicates that the Bell Beaker phenomenon emerged in the Iberian Peninsula, from here, spreading into the central Mediterranean, Central Europe, and Britain and Ireland by 2500 BC. It may also be the case that the first Beaker communities in Europe emerged around the Tagus Estuary in Portugal.

The appearance of the Corded Ware and Beaker Cultures also coincides with a significant change in prehistoric European society, as there was a

shift away from the long-established practice of collective burial in megalithic tombs and caves to one of single burial (although the former was still
favoured by Beaker Culture communities in western and southern France,
and Iberia). It now became more common for single burials to be placed
below circular mounds of earth or stone, and these burials honoured individuals, rather than what could be termed 'communities of ancestors'.
Although the evidence for the settlements and day-to-day lives of Corded
Ware and Beaker communities is scarce, thousands of their burials have been
found across Europe some of which provide us with strong skeletal evidence
that warfare had a part to play in Corded Ware and Beaker society. The male
burials of the Corded Ware and Beaker Cultures also contain weapons that
arguably provide us with the first real signs for the existence of separate
warrior classes or 'institutions' in prehistoric Europe during the third millennium B.C. Rick Schulting has argued that although these burials present
us with idealised images of maleness, these images have some foundation in
reality, otherwise there would be little point in alluding to them.[3]

If we accept that warriorhood was a significant feature of life in the
Corded Ware and Beaker cultures of the Late Neolithic in Europe, we can
never say for sure how the male groups from these two cultures, who specialised in warfare, were organised. Nevertheless, it could be that Corded Ware
and Beaker warriors were drawn from an elite sector of Late Neolithic society, with those of the Beaker Culture perhaps ranked in importance according to age.[4] This 'age-grading' of warriors has been recorded amongst some
non-state societies such as the Loikop/Samburu of northern Kenya, where
warriors were graded by age into junior and senior groups, and who carried
different types of spears to mark their group affiliation.

It may even be the case that some Corded Ware and Beaker warriors used
the horse as a 'tool' of war, although if so, 'cavalry' charges seem unlikely,
and, like the famous Plains Indians of North America, they may have used
their horses to carry them into and away from battles fought on foot. It has
to be admitted, though, that the evidence is somewhat lacking for the use
of the horse in Corded Ware and Beaker warfare. This was an idea favoured
by earlier archaeologists of the 'Culture-Historical School' (most notably
by V. Gordon Childe), who painted a picture of nomadic Corded Ware and
Beaker communities expanding rapidly and aggressively across Europe,
their mounted warriors to the fore. Nonetheless, horse bones have been
found at some Corded Ware and Beaker sites: for example, at the Corded
Ware settlement (dated to 2660–2470 BC) of Wattendorf-Motzenstein in
Franconia, and at the Beaker settlement (c. 2400 BC) that was discovered

adjacent to the famous Newgrange passage grave in County Meath, Ireland. Most scholars probably view such finds as providing evidence that Corded Ware and Beaker communities used horses for agricultural work, and also as sources of food (it is probable that horses were first domesticated to provide a source of winter meat). Perhaps though we should not totally discount the possibility that in some areas of Europe at least, horses were ridden by Corded Ware and Beaker warriors.

Recent archaeological evidence suggests that horses were first domesticated in the steppes of Kazakhstan and Russia, possibly as early as 4500 BC, but definitely by 3500 BC, and the tradition of tribal raiding on horseback could date back to this time. Support for this idea may be provided by the Late Neolithic Suvorovo group (named after a cemetery found in southern Moldova), who probably came from the steppe region around the Lower Dnieper River in Ukraine. Evidence for this group has been found in what appear to be immigrant graves (dating to c. 4300–4100 BC) in the lower Danube Valley, which contained typical Suvorovo artefacts such as polished stone maces carved to resemble horse heads. As these graves appear just before many Bulgarian tell settlements were abandoned, then mounted raiding could have played a part in the collapse of the Late Neolithic Karanovo Culture/society in Bulgaria. Whatever the truth, as we saw in Chapter One, evidence found at some of the Late Neolithic tell settlements of Bulgaria certainly reveals that their abandonment was associated with episodes of destruction and extreme violence.

'Warrior Paraphernalia' in Corded Ware and Beaker Culture Burials

Alongside the distinctive Corded Ware pottery, another characteristic feature of male Corded Ware burials are the striking stone and antler shaft hole mace heads and stone 'battle-axes' that often accompany the deceased (Fig. 8). These objects are often finely made (many are in fact, boat-shaped) and several scholars have plausibly argued that these implements were chiefly made to kill people. For example, Helle Vankilde has stated that: 'The elegantly shaped shaft hole axes and mace heads obviously did not merely symbolise maleness as opposed to femaleness since less than half the males carried them. They surely signified a superior kind of maleness, which included an identity as a warrior. Hunting is less likely inasmuch as the selected weaponry is clearly war-related: it makes no sense to hunt with a mace head or a battle-axe!'[5] Similarly, Andrew Sherrat argued that the battle-axes of the Corded Ware Culture 'are charged with meaning, for they express the ideal of a society whose self-image was not work but warfare'.[6] Jakob Westermann has made the interesting suggestion that Corded Ware maces and battle-axes could be 'associated with the (ritual) slaughtering of animals',[7] but it could also be argued that is quite possible (if not probable) that they were used in the 'ritual slaughter' of enemy captives also.

A common theory is that the pots with cord impression or herring-bone pattern, which feature predominantly in Corded Ware burials, were used in a drinking ritual by warriors, and many archaeologists have also surmised that that Bell Beakers were used in a similar way. In fact, although (unsurprisingly) limited, evidence for alcoholic beverages has been found in some Beakers. For example, there is the well-known Scottish example that was deposited in a cist-grave at Ashgrove Farm, Fife, which probably contained a honey-based mead. Three 'Maritime' beakers that had once contained beer have also been found in a burial mound in Spain (Túmolo de la Sima, Soria) and evidence for a 'super-charged' Beaker beverage containing both beer and the alkaloid, hyoscyamine was identified in one of the Beaker graves found in the Spanish cave-site of Calvari d' Amposta, Tarragona. Hyoscyamine is only found in certain plants and is highly psychotropic (i.e. it causes altered states of consciousness), and hallucinations and euphoria are just two of its many side effects. Some archaeologists have also suggested (perhaps rather imaginatively) that twisted strands of the cannabis plant may have been used to decorate some Corded Ware and Beaker vessels.

Turning to the possible weapons of war found in Beaker burials, males were also sometimes interred with stone axes that are somewhat similar in appearance to Corded Ware battle-axes. Although battle-axes are not particularly common in Beaker graves, given their similarity to Corded Ware ones, it can again be argued that they were not designed with a peaceful purpose in mind, and were first and foremost, weapons of war. In fact, it could be argued that the design and weight of Beaker axes implies that they were for use in close-quarters combat, where they would be particularly effective in dealing out lethal blows to people's heads and upper bodies. Much the same could be said for the Corded Ware battle-axes, even though these are often more elaborately shaped.

Much more ubiquitous in male Beaker burials are the finely made, bifacial (worked on both sides by a technique known as 'pressure flaking') flint barbed and tanged arrowheads, and the evidence seems to be weighted more in favour of the idea that they were probably designed primarily for warfare. Lending some support to this theory is the fact that these arrowheads resemble those used specifically for warfare by some stateless societies such as the Dani of Highland New Guinea, whose war arrowheads were barbed to hinder their removal, and which were coated with mud or grease to increase the chances of deadly infection. Nineteenth century accounts of the arrowheads used by the Great Plains Indians of North America, paint a similar picture, with two types of arrowheads: one for killing wild animals, the other for killing humans. The arrows for killing humans were generally poisoned and featured long barbs, in contrast to the ones used to hunt game, which had inverted barbs, allowing them to be easily extracted and used on future hunting expeditions. It is interesting to note that the rise to dominance of barbed and tanged arrowheads as the main projectile weapon of the Late Neolithic, comes at a time where more deaths and injuries were being caused by archers. It is also something of a paradox, that these arrowheads became prominent at a time when domesticated crops and livestock were the main means of subsistence rather than hunting.

Roger Mercer, however, has interestingly proposed that barbed and tanged arrowheads were chiefly used in ritual hunting forays carried out by a Beaker elite rather than warfare – drawing attention to the aurochs skeleton (dating to the Late Neolithic or Early Bronze Age) found during the excavations that took place in advance of the expansion of Heathrow airport in the 1980s.[8] Barbed and tanged arrowheads were found amongst its ribs and in the area of the animal's pelvis; and two of the arrowheads also displayed impact fractures, indicating that they had penetrated its flesh and hit bone. However, while it is clear that hunting – ritual or otherwise – was still carried out to some extent by Beaker communities, the cumulative evidence still arguably suggests that it is more likely that barbed and tanged arrowheads were projectiles, whose main purpose was to kill people rather than wild animals.

Also found with male Beaker burials are the rather intriguing, flat or plano-convex (flat on one side and curved on the other) rectangular plates of polished stone, which feature two or more perforations at their narrow ends (Fig. 9). These artefacts have traditionally been interpreted as archer's bracers or wrist guards that were worn on the inner wrist to protect against the lash of the bowstring. However, the evidence perhaps indicates that it is more likely that rather being functional objects worn by archers, they were actually ornamental ones. This possibility has been raised by Harry Fokkens et al., who have drawn attention to the fact that Beaker bracers seem to be more often than not, located next to the outer arms of the deceased in graves, suggesting that they were mounted on leather or hide cuffs, where they would be more visible (Fig. 10).[9] They have also pointed out that the ethnographic record shows that many non-state societies used bracers made of leather and hide, and that stone examples are virtually unknown as they are functionally impractical. Bracers made from wood, and even grass, are also known in the ethnographic record, and thus the possible use of Beaker bracers made from organic materials should also be considered. Of course, such bracers are highly unlikely to survive in the archaeological record of Neolithic Europe. With the ornamental idea in mind, it could be possible that the fine quality examples capped with gold rivets, which have been found in a limited number of Beaker burials (e.g. at Driffield, Yorkshire, and Culduthel Mains, Inverness-shire) were used by the top rank of the Beaker 'archer class' to denote their status, with the lesser examples presumably worn by lower ranking warriors.[10] Jan Turek agrees with the ornamental theory, but has also made the interesting suggestion that the design of Beaker bracers meant that they could also be turned into wrist-guards as and when needed.[11] However Beaker bracers were worn on the arm, it is also likely that some examples were 'ceremonial' in nature and were never actually used as functional objects, instead, being made solely for the grave.

Intriguingly, as Turek further points out, bracers have also been found in a limited number of female Beaker burials from Bohemia and Bavaria. It may be that these women were members of the Beaker ruling class, and the inclusion of bracers in their burials is simply a reflection of this, but it is not impossible that they were actual warriors involved in warfare. Admittedly, the skeletal evidence from Beaker burials (and indeed from those of Neolithic Europe in general) suggests that it was men who primarily fought and died in warfare, but as well as the famous Amazons of ancient Greek mythology, there are other instances of females fighting in non-state warfare. For example, small numbers of women joined the war parties of the Crow and Navaho Indians. Similarly, in the Marshall Islands of the Pacific Ocean, it is known that women not only fought to defend their home ground from the enemy, but small numbers of female warriors were also often included in the raiding parties that were sent out to attack enemies.

In addition to ethnographic evidence from pre-state societies, we also have remarkable archaeological evidence for female warriors from the *kurgans* (burial mounds) of the famous Scythians who lived in the central Eurasian steppes from around the ninth to first century BC. In fact, about one-third of all Scythian women found by archaeologists in the *kurgans* were buried with weapons and many have also been found to have war injuries similar to men. This evidence from the steppes, perhaps suggests that the Amazons may not have been the mythical figures of the ancient Greek imagination after all. It may also be interesting to note that Rebecca Redfern's analysis of eighty Late Iron Age (first century BC to first century AD) skulls from the Maiden Castle and Poundbury hillforts (Dorset), identified many blunt and sharp projectile injuries (most of which were lethal) on both male and female skulls, and that roughly equal numbers of males and females had received these injuries.[12] Redfern's conclusion that both sexes had thus fought and died in battles with other Iron Age communities, or perhaps even against Vespasian's *Legio II Augusta*, is thus not an unreasonable one. Such ethnographic and archaeological evidence may indicate that we should not be too ready to totally write women warriors out of the story of Neolithic Europe. At the least, the possibility that women sometimes fought alongside men when defending their villages and families against enemy raiding parties should be considered.

Whatever the truth is about the 'Bell Beaker Amazons', it is quite possible that Beaker bracers had no connection whatsoever with archery, as Anne Woodward and her colleagues have proposed that these objects may actually have been worn by prestigious Beaker falconers to signal their status.[13] Possible evidence to support the bracer hunting theory is known from some Beaker burials, such as the one discovered Kelleythorpe (Driffield, East Yorkshire) in 1851. Here, during 'excavations' conducted by Lord Londesborough, a skeleton lying in a typical flexed position was found in a stone cist grave beneath a barrow. Along with a Beaker and copper dagger, there was a fine quality bracer (featuring two gold-capped rivets on each end) located on the upper right arm bones of the deceased; lying just below and to the right of the bracer, on the floor of the grave, there was a hawk's skull (which has unfortunately now been lost). However, Beaker burials such as this are uncommon, and Robert Wallis (who is both an archaeologist and falconer) has convincingly argued that the stone bracers of the Beaker Culture are much more likely to provide proof of archery rather than falconry.[14]

Not surprisingly, the actual bows used by the putative Beaker archer 'class' are lacking from Beaker graves, and we have only been left with faint traces of their existence (i.e. dark, curved stains in the earth, or small, inconclusive fragments of wood). However, it is interesting to note that miniature pendants made from bone, antler or boars' tusks, which resemble the composite bows used in places such as ancient Egypt and Mesopotamia, have been found in some Beaker graves in Central Europe. It seems, however, to judge from burial evidence, that the battle-axe was the preferred weapon of war in the Corded Ware Culture, although evidence for the use of the composite bow by its communities is not unknown. For example, the decorated side slab of an early Corded ware cist grave found at Leuna-Göhlitzsch in Saxony-Anhalt, Germany, features a carved depiction of what appears to be a composite bow hanging up next to a quiverful of arrows. Behind these weapons, textiles or matting with geometric patterns appear to adorn the wall. The burnt remains of a probable composite bow were also identified in a Corded Ware grave (possibly containing a female) that was discovered at Bo ejewice in Poland. As Miller et al. have noted, composite bows (which combine layers of horn, wood and sinew) were commonly used in ancient Near Eastern warfare, and there is also iconographic evidence from the ancient Near East depicting soldiers using composite bows in both close-quarter combat and in siege warfare.[15]

One of the above probable bow pendants was found in a Beaker cist-grave at the famous megalithic necropolis at the site of Petit-Chasseur in Sion, the capital of the southern canton of Valais, Switzerland. This remarkable late prehistoric cemetery was in use for some fifteen hundred years, with people burying their dead in its megalithic dolmens and stone cists from the Late Neolithic to the Early Bronze Age (c. 2700–2150 BC). However, of more interest to us, is one of the beautifully decorated anthropomorphic stone stele associated with the Beaker reuse of this internationally renowned site (there are thirty-one stelae in total with type A associated with the Late Neolithic use of the necropolis, and type B with the Beaker). This stele or statue-menhir, could quite possibly feature a depiction of a warrior-archer of the Beaker culture, although of course, it could be that we are not looking at a representation of a real figure on the Petit-Chausseur stele. Instead, it could be possible that this, and the other stelae found at the site, represent ancestor figures or guardian deities who watched over the dead. However, whatever the truth is, the carved decoration on its surface provides further evidence for the importance of archery during the time of the Beaker Culture.

Although schematic in nature, the beautifully carved decoration on the Petit-Chasseur stele shows a probable male figure with a bow slung across his chest; his hands are clasped across his waist and he is dressed in a garment featuring the triangle and lozenge patterns that were commonly used to decorate Bell Beakers; a necklace and belt are also depicted (Fig. 11). It could perhaps be possible, as Richard Osgood and Sarah Monks have suggested that the decorated garment is actually 'quilted armour' designed to protect against the arrows of enemy archers.[16] They have further noted that there are many examples of this type of armour in the ethnographic record, and that it may have last been used in action at the battle of Omdurman in Sudan (2 September 1898), where General Kitchener's army defeated the Mahdist army of Abdullah al-Taashi. In New Guinea, warriors of the Tifalmin people, protected themselves from the spears and arrows of their enemies by making cuirasses or corselets from plaited rattan (palm stems).

It may be harder to argue the case that the copper and flint 'daggers' found in some Beaker graves were weapons of war used for stabbing people in close-quarter combat, because several scholars have argued that their generally small size, sharp edges, and rounded points, indicates that they were actually knives. Roger Mercer has suggested that Beaker knives could have been used to administer the *coup de grace* to wounded animals that had been brought down in the ritual hunts carried out by Beaker archers, and that the blood of these animals may then have been drunk from Beaker pots.[17] This is certainly a possibility, but it is equally possible that human as well as animal throats were slit by Beaker knives, with Beaker warriors using them to finish off wounded enemies.

Also of some interest is a small group of Beaker Culture graves (c. 70 in total), which are concentrated in northern and central Jutland, Denmark. In these Danish 'archery graves' (which date from c. 2400–2000 BC) men were buried with beautifully made barbed and tanged arrowheads and flint knives/daggers. The latter are extremely large (averaging 25.2 cm in length, with some examples reaching 44 cm), and represent an impressive testimony to the skills of Late Neolithic flint knappers. These superb artefacts were probably not tools used in daily life (most examples are very thin and delicate), but rather, were made solely for the grave, and like the arrowheads, probably functioned as male symbols of warriorhood.

Also associated with the Beaker culture in Europe (although their origins may date back to the later fourth millennium BC) are the so-called 'halberds', which take their name from the historical halberds (also known as 'pole-arms') that were used to deadly effect by many European armies of the Middle Ages (they are still used today as ceremonial weapons, most notably by the Papal Swiss Guard of the Vatican,). The prehistoric halberd basically consists of an oversize triangular metal blade of copper or bronze that is attached to a long wooden shaft or pole by metal rivets, with the blade sticking out at a right angle.

Some archaeologists are of the opinion that these odd-looking objects (which somewhat resemble the heads of storks or cranes) were not used in combat, and argue that they were ceremonial in nature rather than vicious weapons. However, edge damage observed on some examples appears to suggest otherwise. Furthermore, Ronan O'Flaherty's experiments with a replica of an Irish copper halberd, and several sheep heads, led him to conclude that it was a very effective weapon, and that the blade was designed for impact on human bone (in particular, skulls) rather than muscle.[18] He has also plausibly suggested that halberds were used by warrior champions in one-on-one duels, with individuals showing off their skills and courage during these duels. In fact, some support for this idea may be provided by the possible depiction of halberd 'battles' in the famous prehistoric rock-art of Mont Bégo in the Maritime Alps on the French-Italian border, which consists of many thousands (c. 25,000–30,000) of engraved images broadly dating from the Late Neolithic to the Early/Middle Bronze Age. In fact, there are numerous depictions of single halberds and male figures holding aloft halberds that are over-exaggerated in size, as if to draw attention to their special significance and many carvings of daggers can also be seen. Like the halberds, it seems unlikely that these daggers were symbols of maleness because they were useful utilitarian items.

Skeletal Evidence for Warfare in the Corded Ware and Beaker Cultures

One of the most notable discoveries in respect of Corded Ware warfare was made fairly recently (2005) at a large gravel quarry at Eulau, near the town of Naumburg (Saxony-Anhalt) in Germany. Archaeologists discovered four carefully dug and closely grouped Corded Ware graves (three of which were surrounded by ring ditches c. 6 m in diameter) dating to c. 2650 BC, and each grave contained more than one individual: In grave 99 there was a man and a woman (age 40–60 and 35–50 years respectively), who were accompanied by two children aged about five and nine years old, while Grave 98 contained a woman (30–38 years) and three children aged around one, five, and eight years old. A man (25–40 years) and two children (c. 5 and 6 years of age) were interred in Grave 93, while Grave 90 held the remains of a woman aged around thirty years of age and a child aged about five. Poignantly, some of the individuals faced and held each other in death, with their arms and hands interlinked, and later DNA analysis revealed that Grave 99 contained a husband and wife and their two children. This analysis also indicated that two of the three children in Grave 98 were very probably siblings, although it also suggested that the woman accompanying them was not their mother (as perhaps did the fact that the woman had been buried facing away from them).

However, it is not the evidence for close genetic relationships that is the most interesting aspect of these burials (at least from our point of view), but rather, the traumatic injuries that are evident on some skeletons. The most notable of these was the flint arrowhead found firmly lodged in the spine (fourth lumbar vertebra) of the woman in Grave 90, and it also seems highly unlikely that a second arrowhead found between her ribs on the left side was a grave offering. The man found in Grave 99 had healed injuries on the bones of his left arm and hand, and unhealed injuries on the bones of both his right and left hands. A severe fracture seen on his skull probably caused his death, although it may be possible that this was post-mortem damage caused by soil pressure. However, this seems less likely given that the boy also found in the grave had a serious unhealed wound on the back of his skull, which must have killed him. Likewise, the woman buried in Grave 98 was also clubbed to death, as revealed by the two, large unhealed fractures located towards the top of her skull on the right-hand side. The man from Grave 93 had healed injuries on his left arm and hand, and unhealed injuries on both his right arm and hand. Like his counterpart in Grave 99, he had probably received the latter as he had unsuccessfully tried to defend himself from the lethal intentions of his attacker.

Although no signs of violence were found on the other individuals in the Eulau burials, it appears likely that all thirteen individuals died in a violent enemy attack. Given the careful nature of the burials and the inclusion of grave goods (i.e. stone axes, flint tools, animal tooth pendants and food offerings – the latter revealed by butchered animal bones also found in the graves) in the burials, it also seems likely that friendly hands buried the dead. In fact, teenagers and younger men were not found in the graves and it may be that they returned to their village to perform this grim task, perhaps even burying members of their own families in the process. However, it could be possible that these missing members of the community were taken captive by the raiders, or even killed elsewhere, with their bodies simply left to rot where they lay

An unusual Corded Ware burial in the neighbouring state of Lower Saxony is also worthy of mention here. This was found near the village of Bavenstedt, where archaeologists excavated a Corded Ware cemetery featuring seven graves (c. 2500 BC). In contrast to the normal Corded Ware burial rite, one of the graves contained the skeletons of two men who had been buried side by side, the right hand of one man resting on the left shoulder of the other, with the latter lying unusually on his back (the dead were normally placed in flexed positions in Corded Ware graves). This burial anomaly can probably be explained by the flint arrowhead that was still stuck in his spinal column (between his eighth and ninth thoracic vertebrae), and the post-traumatic paraplegia that the man must have suffered as result. He probably soon died from the bacterial meningitis that was caused by this arrow injury, although it may be possible that he actually died after having received a severe soft tissue wound, perhaps from a dagger. His companion in the grave was also found with an arrowhead in the stomach region, with the arrow probably perforating the intestines and causing massive internal haemorrhages. He would not have survived this injury for long, and at best, lived for a few days after being shot. It is likely that the two men received their fatal injuries at the same time, and it is also possible that these injuries are related to an episode of warfare between rival Corded Ware communities.

Further probable evidence for warfare amongst Corded Ware communities comes from the site of Vikletice in the north-western part of the Czech Republic, which represents the largest Corded Ware cemetery yet discovered (around 170 graves). Six of the males found here had signs of violent blows to the left side of the head, and this presumably indicates that these (probably fatal) wounds had been delivered by battle-axes wielded by warriors who were predominantly right-handed. Jonas Cristensen has also noted that demographic analysis of the cemetery revealed that men aged 15–30 'died 15 per cent more frequently than they should have done naturally [and that] the most likely explanation for the high mortality rate among young men is warfare'.[19]

Perhaps the most notable 'casualty of war' from the Beaker Culture was discovered at Stonehenge in April 1978 by Cardiff University's Department of Archaeology, who were carrying out a series of small-scale excavations at the world-famous monument, largely in order to obtain data on the prehistoric environment at the time of its construction. The archaeologists must therefore have been rather surprised, and probably rather thrilled, to discover a crude grave containing the skeleton of a young adult male (aged 25–30) in the outer ditch surrounding the monument (this ditch was actually built about 500 years before the mighty sarsen trilithons and Welsh bluestones were raised at the site). He lay in the grave in a flexed position, and the barbed and tanged arrowheads discovered amongst his ribs and a stone bracer also discovered in the grave (close to his left arm), identified him as a member of the Beaker Culture (Fig. 12). In the initial short report on the discovery, the possibility that the arrowheads were the cause of death was – somewhat oddly, given their location amongst his bones – not considered. However, later scientific analysis revealed that the man had been shot at close-range, probably by more than one attacker, and that in fact, he was killed by at least four and possibly more arrows, with the death-dealing arrowhead probably passing through his heart. The three arrowheads had broken tips, with one tip discovered in the sternum and another in one of the ribs. Whether this young man was a casualty of war remains a matter of debate, and it could be that he was chosen as a sacrificial victim, whose life was violently cut short in honour of a powerful Neolithic deity or deities c. 2300 BC. However, with this theory in mind, it could be that he was a captured prisoner of war, or alternatively, he may have been someone who had fought bravely, but lost his life in combat and was subsequently given a place of honour at this prestigious monument.

The fame of the 'Stonehenge Archer', however, was eclipsed nearly a quarter of a century later (2002), when the 'Amesbury Archer' was discovered lying in one of the most richly furnished Beaker graves in Europe, on Boscombe Down some 4.5 km to the south-east of Stonehenge. The grave contained the burial of an adult male (35–45 years old) who had probably been lain to rest (c. 2350 BC) in a wooden burial chamber, and he was accompanied by a remarkable collection of grave goods. Included amongst these were: five Bell Beakers, two fine quality bracers, one made from a dark grey stone (this was located on the outside of the lower left forearm), probably of continental origin, the other from a striking red stone perhaps originating in Pembrokeshire, three copper knives or daggers (that may have been made in northern Spain or western France), a probable shale belt ring, and a 'cushion stone' used for making small metal objects, and four boars' tusks. Several flint tools including two well-made knives/daggers, were also found with the Archer, an antler pin, and two small and sheet-gold basket ornaments that may have been worn as either earrings or tress-rings in braided hair. There were also seventeen finely made barbed and tanged arrowheads, which had probably been hafted when originally placed in the grave (as indeed was probably the case in many other arrowheads found in other European Beaker burials).

Although there were no obvious signs that the Amesbury Archer had been violently killed, he was missing his left capella or kneecap. This may possibly have been because he suffered from a rare congenital condition known as 'small patella syndrome', but lesions in the knee-joint could indicate that the Archer suffered a severe blow that shattered his knee-cap. Alternatively, an injury might have been caused by a direct blow or a fall, and perhaps the

Archer was even thrown from a horse travelling at speed, as may have been the case with a well-healed, but major fracture, seen on the left femur an adult male found in the grave of the 'Boscombe Bowmen'. This unusual (at least in Britain) multiple Beaker burial was found only about 0.5 km (miles) from that of the Amesbury Archer on Boscombe Down. It contained the remains of nine to ten individuals who were buried around the same time as their more illustrious neighbour with various artefacts including eight Beakers, a possible antler bow pendant, and five barbed and tanged arrowheads.

Whatever the cause of his absent patella, it could be that the Amesbury Archer was given such a prestigious burial because he was a metalworker, who must have been seen as esoteric and 'magical' figures when metal objects first began to be made in the later Neolithic. Alternatively, he may have been given a special burial because he had undertaken a 'heroic' journey from his homeland (scientific analysis of the archer's teeth indicated that he was born in Central Europe, probably somewhere in the Alpine region). However, Jakob Westermann has argued that the placing of the objects in the Archer's grave suggests that he was a person of some power, who had various craftsmen under his patronage, and that this power had been gained through his role as a warrior.[20] Whatever the true role of the Amesbury Archer in life, there can be little doubt that he was a person of considerable importance, although it is highly unlikely that he was the 'King of Stonehenge' as the popular press dubbed him soon after his discovery.

Although it is probably unlikely (but not impossible) that the Amesbury Archer was killed in combat, other Beaker Culture burials found elsewhere in Britain and continental Europe are more suggestive in this respect. For instance, at the Sarn-y-Bryn-Caled timber circle near Welshpool, Powys, four barbed and tanged arrowheads were found amongst the cremated remains of an individual who had been buried in a pit in the centre of the circle probably at the end of the Late Neolithic/beginning of the Early Bronze Age c. 2200 BC. Although they had been turned white or 'calcined' by the fierce heat of the funeral pyre, the fact that two examples had their tips missing but were otherwise intact, strongly indicates that all the arrows had been lodged in the body of the individual prior to his cremation. In one of the graves uncovered at the Staxton Beaker cemetery, Yorkshire, a male skeleton displayed evidence that the individual buried here had received a serious and probably lethal blow to his left shoulder from a weapon of some sort (a battle-axe?). The skeleton of a young man who had probably been killed by an archer was found beneath a Beaker barrow excavated at Fordington Farm found near Dorchester. A lone barbed and tanged arrowhead was found lying on his pelvis, and given its location, it seems more probable that it was an instrument of death rather than a grave good.

Heading to continental Europe, and the mountainous region of Dosrius near Barcelona, there is the Costa de Can Martorell 'hypogea' (rock-cut tomb), which yielded the remains of nearly two hundred individuals. As well as an 'Epimaritime' Beaker, sixty-one barbed and tanged arrowheads were found scattered in the tomb, many of which displayed impact fractures that can only have been caused by them hitting solid objects. It is highly likely that these 'objects' were actually the people buried in the hypogea, and the fact that most of them were buried simultaneously points strongly towards a massacre or battle in which many individuals lost their lives. Similar evidence has been found at the two megalithic tombs of Can Gol I and II in Catalonia, which interestingly, are located less than 10 km from the Costa de Can Martorell hypogea. Both tombs (which lie less than 500 m apart) were excavated in 1946, and four barbed and tanged arrowheads were recovered from Can Gol I, as well as fragmentary human remains, sherds from five Bell Beakers, and two pendants of stone and shell. Can Gol II yielded three barbed and tanged arrowheads, and a few flint tools, although no human remains were recorded. Six of these arrowheads have recently been closely examined by Ignacio Soriano and colleagues.[21] They concluded from their analysis that four of the arrowheads 'exhibit highly probable impact fractures linked with their use as projectiles' and that their results 'were sufficient to confirm the existence of an episode of violence linked to the Bell Beaker culture'. Soriano et al. have also argued that this violence took the form of 'a rare, short-lived skirmish', rather than a more serious outbreak of open warfare in which significant numbers of people were killed. This is possible in the case of Can Gol I and II, but the evidence found at Costa de Can Martorell suggests that such warfare was not unknown in this corner of north-east Spain during the time of the Beaker Culture. In any case, history has repeatedly shown that skirmishes are part and parcel of, and often the prelude to, full-blown and significant warfare.

Chapter 4

France and Italy

In recent years, two important archaeological discoveries from the Alsace border region of north-eastern France have provided further strong evidence that warfare had more than a minor role to play in European Neolithic society. The first was made by ANTEA-Archéologie, during a rescue excavation conducted at the site of Bergheim, located some 35 miles south-east of Strasbourg in the Haut-Rhin department of Alsace. Along with evidence for LBK houses and an area of grain silos or circular pits dating to the Iron Age, sixty Neolithic silos were also discovered, with fourteen of these yielding human remains, with one silo in particular (pit 157) standing out from the others. At the base of this 2 metre-deep pit, the French archaeologists discovered the upper arm bones of seven individuals and the bones from the hands of at least five people. Six of the arm bones belonged to adults, with the other belonging to a youth aged 12–16 years. Closer examination of the bones revealed numerous fractures and chop marks, which are related to amputations probably carried out with a stone axe/s and the secondary cutting up of the arms and hands. Directly overlying these amputated bones, there were the remains of seven people and a skull cap fragment belonging to an infant probably less than one year old. It was apparent from the haphazard ordering of the bones that the corpses had simply been thrown into the pit and piled on top of one another, with three adults (two males and one female) and four children (aged between 2–5 years) represented by the skeletal material. It was also evident that the lowest individual (number 7) in this funerary deposit, who was a mature male aged between 30 and 60 years of age, had five fractures which were the result of severe blows to his skull. If not dead already at the time that these blows were rained down on is head, they would have certainly proved fatal. Further evidence of severe blows to the man's left shoulder and ribs were also identified, and his left upper arm had also been amputated; a flint arrowhead was also found in an 'interesting' position near his ribs. Both the upper limbs and the complete individuals found in pit 157 were deposited together at the same, or within a very short space of time, with radiocarbon dates taken from the bones indicating that the amputated limbs and corpses had been dumped in the pit between c. 4300–4000 BC.

The second discovery was made at the Achenheim Neolithic enclosure on the outskirts of Strasbourg, which is being investigated by archaeologists from France's National Institute for Preventative Archaeology (INRAP). Located inside the enclosure, which is surrounded by a deep V-shaped ditch, that features what have been interpreted as defensive 'bastions' at its entrances, the French team have discovered three hundred subterranean pits or silos used by the Neolithic inhabitants of the site for storing grain and other foodstuffs. Inside one of these (silo 124), were the remains of ten individuals comprising the complete skeletons of five adult males, one adolescent male, and the dismembered arm bones from four other people. The dead had clearly been dumped into the pit (at some point between 4400–4200 BC) without any care, as the skeletons were found lying on their sides, backs, and stomachs, with their bones sometimes intermingled. It was also clear that these people, whose remains had lain hidden in the bottom of the pit for some six thousand years, had many violent fractures on their skulls, legs, hands, feet, and ribs. It would be very hard to argue against the idea that these people were killed brutally in a single event involving extreme violence, and that they had been killed with a stone axe or axes.

Some of the arms of the dead found in the pit had also been severed, and several wounds on the bones also appear to be post-mortem in character, appearing to represent a case of 'overkill', perhaps by warriors who had worked themselves up into a war frenzy. The arm bones comprise the upper left arms of three adults and the left forearm of a youth aged 12–16 years. Although the sex of the people from whom they had been severed (perhaps as they were still alive) has not been ascertained, as at Bergheim, they have been interpreted as arms hacked off as war trophies. Perhaps the most common war trophy taken in non-state warfare was the head or skull of an enemy, and this custom is recorded in many cultures across the world, (headhunting/taking will be discussed in more detail in the final chapter). However, the taking of other body parts as war trophies has been documented in many non-state societies also. For instance, the French artist Jacques Le Moyne de Morgues recorded this practice amongst the Timucua Indians of Florida in the sixteenth century: 'They also are accustomed, after a battle, to cut off with these reed knives the arms of the dead near the shoulders, and their legs near the hips'. Trophy taking was also common amongst the native Eskimo groups of America's North Pacific Rim, and the Russian

Bishop, Ioann Veniaminov, who lived amongst the Aleutians from 1824–1834 (and who converted many of them to the Orthodox Church) described how, following an Aleut raid:

> Those [enemies] destined for captivity were marked with blood spots on the face and on the forehead while the one whom they intended to kill had an ear or some other part of the body cut off, for instance, a part of the scalp. They even cut out the genital organs of men as well as of the women. And those parts cut off or excised out of the body, and the weapons taken from the enemy, were the most important trophies of the victors, who passed them on to their descendants for the glory of their lineage as living memorials of their military exploits; a few of the conquerors ordered that such trophies be put into their graves.[1]

It seems also that the Aleut sometimes found themselves on the receiving end of similar treatment from their enemies. In 1994, archaeologists excavating an Aleut settlement at Peterson Lagoon, Unimak Island, found a skeleton missing its hands, feet, and head, in the side room of a 'barabara' (a semi-subterranean house); a slate projectile point of the neighbouring Koniag people was also found lodged between two of the cervical vertebrae of the skeleton.

Further examples of trophy taking in non-state warfare come from South America and New Zealand, where the long bones of defeated enemies were turned into flutes. Although not used as flute, it may be interesting to note that a human femur, which had been used as a hand-pick, is reported as having been found at the famous Neolithic flint mines at Grimes Graves, Norfolk. It seems unlikely that this thigh bone would have been taken from the skeleton of a loved one, and then used to extract flint from the remarkable underground galleries that still survive today at this famous site. Several tribes in Colombia are known to have flayed the bodies of their defeated enemies, with this practice often performed by women who accompanied the men to the battlefield. One of these Columbian tribes made effigies of their defeated enemies by stuffing these skins, and by crudely modelling in wax the facial features of the dead on their skulls, with weapons also placed in their hands. These effigies were then given places of honour within houses, being set up and displayed on special tables and benches that were made for this purpose. Even more extreme levels of trophy taking were reached in Tahiti, where victorious warriors made trophy 'ponchos' out of the corpses of their enemies by pounding them flat with their heavy war clubs and by then cutting slits in these flattened skins.

The scalping of enemies also represents another form of trophy taking amongst non-state peoples, and has of course become synonymous with the native Indians of North America, even though other non-state societies took the scalps of their enemies. It has been claimed by some historians that it was European settlers who introduced this custom to the native Americans, and scalping was undoubtedly carried out by some settlers, who were offered bounties for Indian scalps (as brilliantly dramatised in *Blood Meridian* by Cormac McCarthy, a dark and violent story based on the real exploits of a group of nineteenth century, professional American scalp-hunters known as the 'Glanton Gang'). However, it is evident from the accounts of early settlers, and from archaeological evidence such as that found at the previously mentioned Crow Creek site, that this was a native practice already well established long before the first Europeans set foot on American soil.

The elite warriors of the Classic Maya civilisation of Mesoamerica (c. 250–1050 AD) cut off the heads of their defeated enemies and carved them into decorated skull masks which would be worn as pectorals, hung from belts, or worn as actual masks. These masks not only celebrated the power of the victors, but were perhaps also believed to be a necessary part of the maintenance of cosmological order in the Maya world. As well as numerous depictions of these skull masks in Maya art, there have been several archaeological discoveries of these trophies. For example, at the site of Pakal Na in the Sibun Valley, Belize, one of the individuals buried in a large grave pit was accompanied by a skull mask featuring a carved mat motif. Clear cut-marks from the flaying of the head of the unfortunate individual whose skull became a trophy, could also be seen on the mask along with drilled holes. At the famous Maya site of Copan, the skeleton of a slim, young man was discovered buried under the staircase of one of the large elite residences, and the skull mask that had been placed on his chest when he was interred in this position of honour was still in place.

A fairly common practice in the Roman army was the decapitation and display of enemy heads, as revealed by the depiction of such heads on the gravestones of Legionaries in northern Britain. A cache of decapitated skulls found at the Roman site of 52–63 London Wall in 1988 may represent enemy heads taken by Roman soldiers stationed in Londinium, which were ritually deposited in the Walbrook Valley. However, it is also possible that they were the heads of gladiatorial victims who had lost their lives in the city's amphitheatre.

It was not just 'primitive' and ancient warriors who took trophies from the bodies of their fallen enemies in warfare, but the soldiers of 'civilised' armies too. For example, during the terrible Pacific War of World War II, American soldiers quite frequently collected body parts as trophies from dead Japanese soldiers. For the most part, these were skulls taken from full or partial skeletonised remains, with many of these 'souvenirs' sent home to their loved ones in the United States. One such skull, which bore many inscriptions and autographs of US soldiers, was found during a drugs raid carried out in the city of Pueblo, Colorado, and was inscribed: 'Guadalcanal, November 11, 1942' (the Battle of Guadalcanal was the first major offensive of the Pacific War and marked a decisive turning point in this conflict). On occasion, however, fully fleshed heads were removed from the Japanese dead, and then boiled to remove the flesh from the skulls. Although occurring less frequently, other body parts other than skulls were also taken from the dead by the US Soldiers. The famous pioneer aviator, Charles Lindbergh (who was a civilian advisor to the US Army and Navy), recorded that a marine officer told him that his men sometimes cut off the ears and noses of dead Japanese soldiers, some of which were dried and taken back to the States. Japanese teeth were also sometimes taken and turned into necklaces, with gold fillings also prised from the dead to be later bartered or sold. Lindbergh also reported that Fighter Control personnel in New Guinea carved the leg bones of dead Japanese soldiers into objects such as letter-openers and pen-holders. During the nineteenth century, British and German soldiers fighting in Africa also sometimes took the skulls (and severed heads) of enemy warriors as trophies.

Exactly who was responsible for the murderous events revealed at Bergheim and Achenheim lies beyond our reach, but it could be that they were carried out by locals against raiders from outside the Alsace region, and the Parisian Basin has been proposed as the area from which these raiders may have come. On the other hand, it may be possible that incomers rather than locals, were the victors, with the latter on the receiving end of extremely vicious treatment by the former. Given the proximity of the two sites and their similar dates, it could perhaps even be possible that the massacres revealed at them were carried out by the same group (archaeologists are planning to carry out isotopic analysis on the bones of the people found in the two pits at Bergheim and Achenheim, which should reveal whether they were locals or incomers). Whatever the true identity of the people who were carelessly dumped in pit 157 and silo 124, their remains indicate that the Alsace region was troubled by warfare at some point in the later French

Neolithic. They also seem to provide further evidence that the defeated in Neolithic warfare, were sometimes treated with extreme brutality by the victorious.

Skeletal Evidence from French Neolithic Funerary Sites

Several Neolithic funerary sites in France have also yielded skeletons displaying traumatic injuries, some of which were obviously the cause of death. Many of these wounds were caused by arrows, and at least some of them must surely have been received in armed conflicts between Neolithic communities. These injuries were first noted on Neolithic skeletons in France by nineteenth century antiquarians (as they were in other parts of Europe such as Britain), at sites such as the cave of Les Baumes-Chaudes in the southern Gévaudan region, where Dr Barthélémy Prunières discovered the skeletal remains of some three to four hundred Late Neolithic people. On examination of these remains, he found that eighteen skeletons in the cave had flint arrows still embedded in their bones, and that a copper dagger was also stuck in the thorax of one individual. It is quite probable that several other people in the cave had also died violently, even though there were no obvious wounds on their skeletons. Dr Prunières found several other Neolithic individuals who had been struck or killed by arrows as did his contemporary, another doctor, Baron de Baye, who for example, recorded a flint arrowhead in a vertebra from the cave-site of Pierre-Michelot (Marne), and another in a tibia recovered from the Font Rial tomb in Aveyron in the Languedoc region. In Villevénard cave, the Baron found another arrowhead lodged between the vertebrae of one skeleton and a skull containing three arrowheads. It seems likely that many – if not all of the seventy-three arrowheads he is recorded as having recovered from another French Neolithic cave-burial, were also probably once lodged in the flesh of the people that were interred in the cave.

Until the recent discoveries made at Bergheim and Achenheim, perhaps the strongest evidence for Neolithic warfare in France came from the famous site of Roaix in the Vaucluse department of south-eastern France. Excavations carried out at this rock-cut tomb in 1965 and 1966 identified two separate layers of dead who had been deposited in the tomb around 2500 BC. Although there were no signs of violence to be found on the skeletons in the lower level, things were somewhat different in the upper one. In the top level (which was unfortunately badly damaged by illegal excavation), the fully articulated skeletons of sixty to seventy men, women, and children had

Fig. 1. Neolithic stone axe from Ehenside Tarn, Cumbria (J. Miall, CC BY-SA 3.0).

Fig. 2. Late Neolithic barbed and tanged arrowhead from the Dolmen de la Glene megalithic tomb, Aveyron, France (Didier Descouens CC BY-SA 3.0).

Fig. 3. The Anasazi 'Cliff Palace', Mesa Verde National Park, Colorado (Andreas F. Borchert, CC BY-SA 3.0).

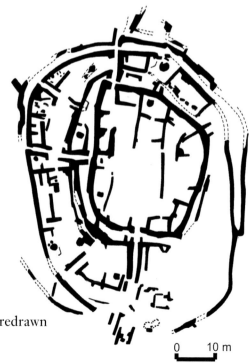

Fig. 4. Plan of Dimini, Greece (redrawn after Papathanassopoulos).

0   10 m

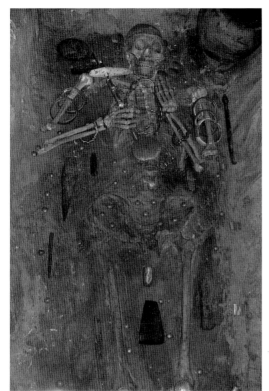

Fig. 5. Reconstructed burial of the Varna 'Chieftain' (Yelkrokoyade CC BY-SA 3.0).

Fig. 6. Linearbandkeramik (LBK) pottery vessel from Bavaria (Wolfgang Sauber CC BY-SA 3.0).

Fig. 7. The Talheim 'Death Pit' (photo courtesy of Prof. Joachim Wahl).

Fig. 8. Corded Ware battle axes in the Museum of Prehistory and Early History, Berlin (Einsamer Schutze, CC BY-SA 3.0).

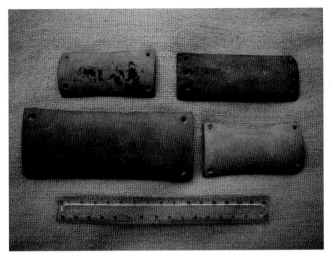

Fig. 9. Beaker bracers from Bohemia (photo courtesy of Dr Jan Turek).

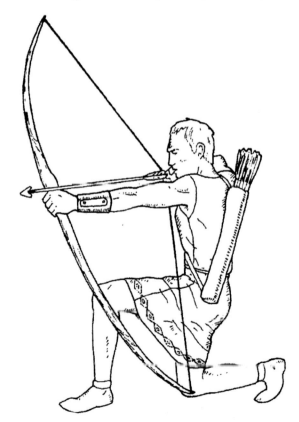

Fig. 10. Beaker archer wearing a bracer in the 'ornamental' position (redrawn after Fokkens et al.).

Fig. 11. The Petit-Chausseur 'Warrior' stelae (photo courtesy of Dr Jan Turek).

Fig. 12. Plan of the 'Stonehenge Archer's' burial (redrawn after Edmonds).

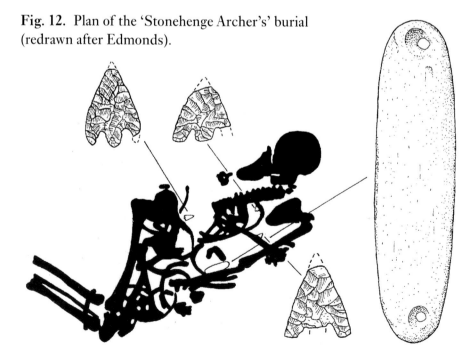

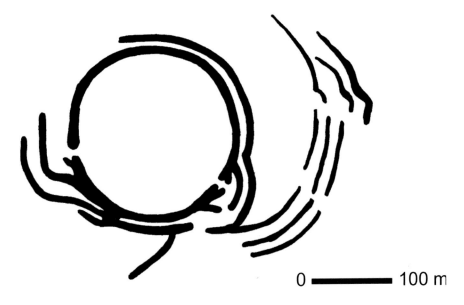

Fig. 13. Plan of the Semussac 'pince de crabe' enclosure, France (redrawn after Scarre).

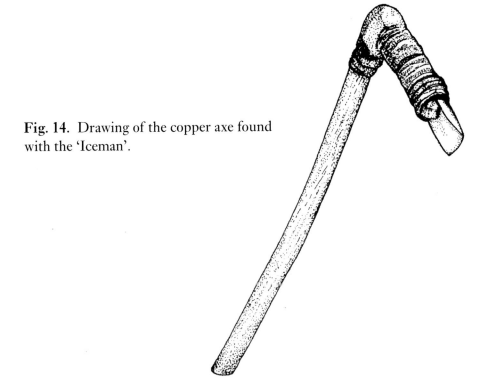

Fig. 14. Drawing of the copper axe found with the 'Iceman'.

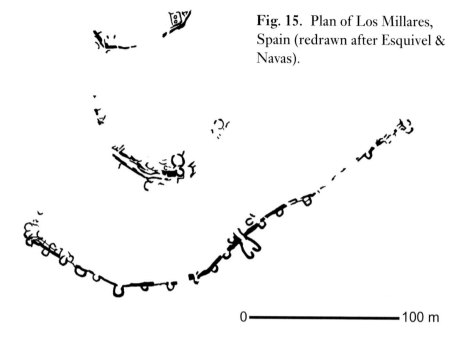

Fig. 15. Plan of Los Millares,
Spain (redrawn after Esquivel &
Navas).

0 ———————————— 100 m

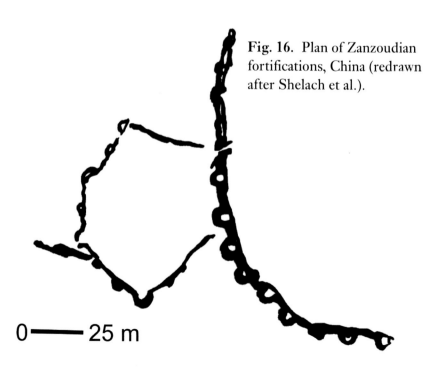

Fig. 16. Plan of Zanzoudian
fortifications, China (redrawn
after Shelach et al.).

0 ——— 25 m

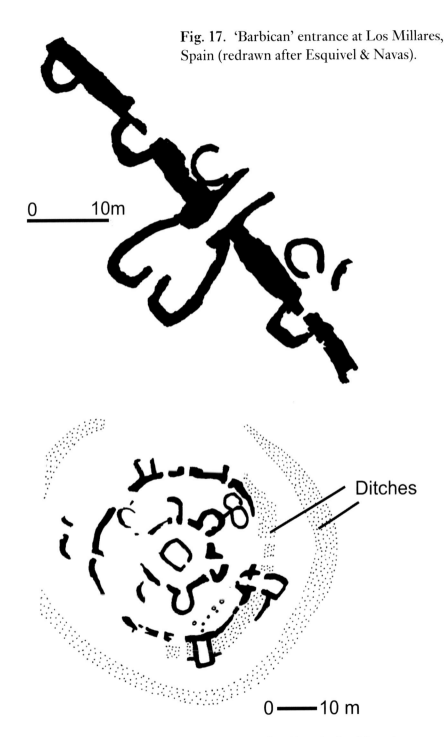

Fig. 17. 'Barbican' entrance at Los Millares, Spain (redrawn after Esquivel & Navas).

0 _____ 10m

Ditches

0 ——— 10 m

Fig. 18. 'Fortin 1', Los Millares (redrawn after Esquivel & Navas).

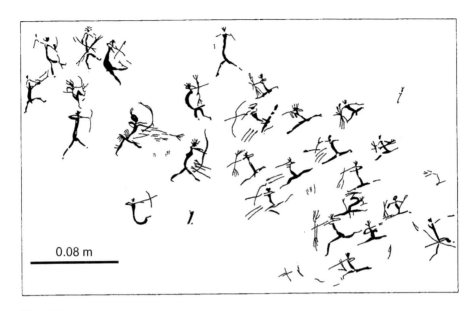

Fig. 19. Depiction of an archery battle from Les Dogues rockshelter, Spain (redrawn after Nash).

Fig. 20. The 'Phalanx', from El Cingle de la Mola Remegia rockshelter, Spain (redrawn after Nash).

Fig. 21. Depiction of an archer with a dead or dying comrade from El Cingle de la Mola Remegia rockshelter, Spain (redrawn after Nash).

Fig. 22. Depiction of a warrior pierced with arrows from El Cingle de la Mola Remegia rockshelter, Spain (redrawn after Nash).

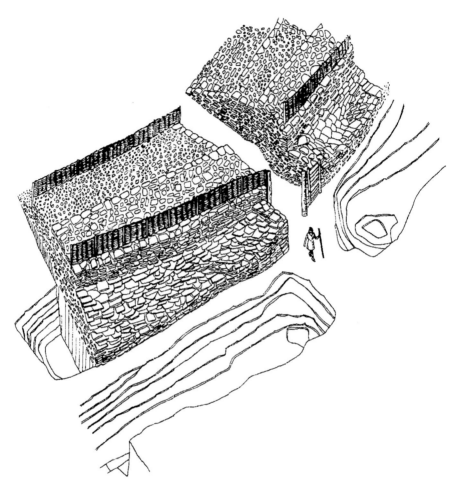

Fig. 23. Reconstruction drawing of the rampart at Crickley Hill
(redrawn after Dixon & Borne).

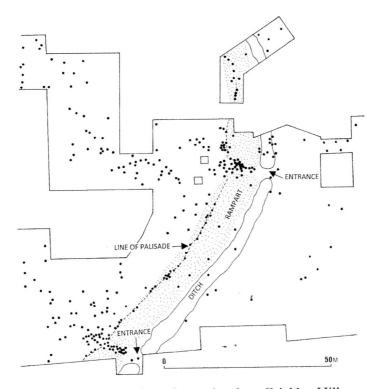

Fig. 24. Plan of the distribution of arrowheads at Crickley Hill (redrawn after Dixon).

Fig. 25. Entrance to Wayland's Smithy Long Barrow (M. Semmett, CC BY-SA 3.0).

Fig. 26. Hambledon Hill, Dorset (Marilyn Peddle, CC BY-SA 3.0).

Fig. 27. Leaf-shaped arrowheads found at Selsey, Sussex (Geni, CC BY-SA 3.0).

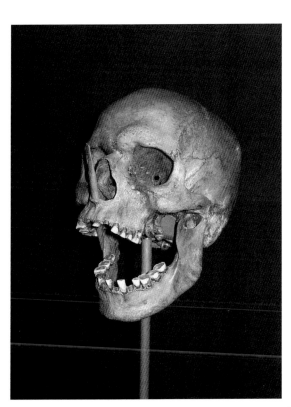

Fig. 28. Drawing of the Meare longbow from Somerset, as found, and reconstructed (redrawn after Coles & Orme).

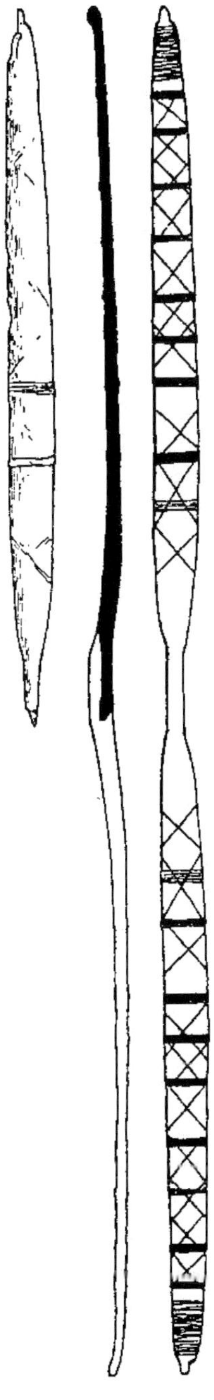

Fig. 29. Male skull with embedded bone arrowhead from Pormose, Denmark (Andreas Franzkowiak, CC BY-SA 3.0).

Fig. 30. Poulnabrone Portal Tomb, Ireland (K. Glavin, CC BY-SA 3.0).

originally been deposited simultaneously, the bodies crowded together, side by side (about 60 per cent of the dead were adults). Lying scattered amongst their skeletons were many flint arrowheads, seven of which were actually embedded in bones. Who these people were, and exactly how they died, lies forever hidden in the Neolithic shadows. However, it is certainly possible, as many archaeologists have suggested, that the upper level of skeletons found at Roaix represent a Neolithic war grave. In fact, given that the skeletons in the upper 'war level' were all deposited at the same time, there is a distinct possibility that it represents the killing of many, if not all of the members of a Neolithic community by an enemy group.

Further examples of deadly violence from French Neolithic funerary sites include that found at the Pontharaud cemetery (dated to c. 4500–4300 BC), Auvergne, where the remains of five men and two adolescents were found in a megalithic tomb. The position of the bones suggested that the bodies had been placed in the tomb at the same time. Although only one man had been killed by an arrow, which was still stuck in his skeleton, it is quite probable that the other individuals were killed alongside him. Individuals who had died as a result of violent blows to the skull are also known from some French Neolithic funerary sites, such as the two young men found at Les Chatelliers du Vieil-Auzy (Vendée), where there were three megalithic tombs each containing double burials of young men or teenagers. One of the men in tomb 4 had a severe fracture on the left parietal bone, towards the back of his skull, while the other (in tomb 3) had received a very violent full-frontal blow to the face, which had badly fractured his jaw and nose, cracked his maxilla (upper jaw), and knocked most of his upper teeth out of his head. This individual also had an arrowhead embedded in his spine, and his 'companion' accompanying him in the tomb had also been killed by an arrowhead.

Although rare, we also have skeletal evidence pointing towards Neolithic armed conflict across the French border in Belgium. In 1865, E. Dupont discovered and excavated a Late Neolithic collective burial at the cave of Trou Rosette, which comprised at least six adults and nine children. Over one hundred years later, during a re-evaluation of prehistoric skeletal material held by the Royal Belgian Institute of Natural Sciences, Caroline Polet and her colleagues identified a deep wound on a fragment of bone from a left adult pelvis. Embedded in this wound was a broken flint arrowhead. It seems that this arrowhead did not immediately kill the individual into whose body it was fired, as the wound had healed, and he/she may have survived for some years following this injury. It is hard to say for sure whether this was a war injury or a hunting accident, but the former nevertheless remains a possibility.

Warfare Cannibalism at Fontbregoua?

The well-known site of Fontbrégoua Cave is located in Provence about 100 km from Marseille and the Mediterranean coast, and was excavated by André Taxil from 1948–1960, with further excavations conducted here by Jean Courtin in the 1970s. These excavations uncovered evidence that the cave was used repeatedly as a seasonal camp by various Neolithic groups between c. 5400–3600 BC, with cultural material such as pottery, stone tools, and carbonized grains recovered from three discrete areas: the porch, the main room, and the lower room (evidence that the cave had also used by Upper Palaeolithic or 'Old Stone Age' hunter-gatherers was also recovered). Also found in the floor of the cave were thirteen clusters of bones, which Neolithic people had placed in shallow, man-made hollows scattered randomly throughout the cave (they were dug between c. 5450–5100 BC). Ten of these were found to contain the butchered remains of wild and domestic animals such as boar, red deer, and sheep, while the other three only contained human bones, comprising the remains of at least twenty-one individuals, with six children and seven adults identified amongst this skeletal material. The excavators of the cave also surmised that there had probably been more clusters of human bone but that these had subsequently been disturbed by later Neolithic occupants of the cave.

Cut marks seen on the animal bones clearly showed that they had been processed for their meat, but there is a strong possibility that it was not just the meat from wild and domestic animals that was being eaten by Neolithic people at Fontebrégoua, but human beings too. This controversial claim was made by Paola Villa and her colleagues, after their subsequent analysis of the human bones recovered from the cave. Writing in the academic journal *Science*, they argued that 'the analysis of these bones strongly suggests that humans were butchered, processed, and probably eaten in a manner that closely parallels the treatment of wild and domestic animals at Fontebrégoua'.[2] It was a bold claim, but it was one that Villa and her colleagues were perfectly entitled to make, for as Karoline Lukaschek has said in her discussion of the skeletal evidence from the cave: 'With respect to cut mark location and morphology [type], a remarkable degree of concordance can be observed between animal and human bones: 70 per cent of the cut mark varieties on the human bones can be matched to similar marks on corresponding animals'.[3] Some of the human long bones also display fractures that are indicative of marrow extraction, and the more extensive defleshing of the human skulls, in contrast to the animal ones, may perhaps be because they were skinned and then kept as trophies or ritual objects. Along with fragments from a stone bracelet, pieces from a broken stone axe were found with one of the human bone clusters (Feature H3), and chop marks seen on a rib and vertebra found in this feature were probably made by this axe.

Unsurprisingly, given the strong feelings that cannibalism engenders among people, not all scholars agree with the hypothesis that the human remains from Fontbrégoua provide evidence of Neolithic cannibalism. Michael Pickering, for example, has argued that they are more likely to represent burial rites rather than cannibalistic activities, drawing on ethnographic accounts of the mortuary rituals of some Australian Aboriginal societies in support of his argument.[4] These accounts showed that after bodies had been left for a while to decompose, the flesh was then cut from their bones for secondary burial. However, taken cumulatively, the skeletal evidence from Fontbrégou arguably weakens Pickering's theory. Furthermore, if it was a non-violent funerary ritual, then it was a very unusual one that does not appear to have been paralleled elsewhere in Neolithic France. Of course, it could be that this evidence represents desperate measures by starving Neolithic people, but this is also improbable as they obviously had access to both wild and domestic animals.

If then, as the evidence more strongly suggests, that both animal and human flesh was being consumed at Fontbrégoua cave, then perhaps the most plausible explanation is that the people at Fontbrégoua were killed in an enemy attack, and afterwards eaten by their attackers in an act of warfare cannibalism. The archaeological jury will probably be forever out on this controversial issue, but this scenario is certainly worth considering, and perhaps best fits the intriguing evidence recovered from Fontbrégoua cave.

Fortified Sites in Western France?

At least 100 Neolithic enclosures are known in western France, and it has been plausibly suggested that there may originally have been as many as 250 enclosures here. As in other parts of Europe, the traditional view of these enclosures is that they were fortified settlements or refuges, which protected Neolithic communities against attack. Today, however, the archaeological consensus is that for the most part, the Neolithic enclosures of western France were not defended sites; rather, they are seen as meeting places where different Neolithic communities met to participate in rituals and ceremonies, which helped to reinforce social links between people. This is a view mirrored by many other archaeologists who study and work on the Neolithic enclosures of Western Europe, and it has to be said that the archaeological evidence recovered from their ditches and interiors lends some support to this idea. However, as we have previously seen, at least some Neolithic enclosures have provided evidence not only of fortification but also of armed attacks, destruction, and violent death, and even possible desecration of the enemy dead in the form of warfare cannibalism.

It is also worth bearing in mind that ritual and ceremonial explanations are not mutually exclusive of defensive ones. For example, there are examples of fortified ceremonial centres in the Andes, such as the Inca shrines of Ancocagua near Cusco, Samaipata in Bolivia, Chankillo in the Casma Valley (which has substantial walls incorporating baffled gates), and Pacatnamú in the Jequetepeque Valley of northern Peru, which is enclosed by triple walls and ditches. A mass grave containing the skeletons of fourteen adolescent and young males was also found at the entrance to a ceremonial precinct at this latter site, which was built by people of the Moche culture (c. 100–800 AD). It was clear that these young men had died horrible deaths, as cut marks seen on their skeletons revealed evidence of multiple stabbings, and decapitation or throat slashing. Five individuals also displayed breakage patterns on their ribs, suggesting that their chest cavities had been forcibly opened in order to remove their hearts. It is quite probable that these young men represent war captives who were ritually sacrificed to Moche gods.

As far as I am aware, no firm evidence for attack and destruction has been found at the Late Neolithic enclosures of western France, but some of these sites do display architectural features to suggest that their builders may have been threatened by hostile neighbours. Perhaps the strongest candidate in this regard is the well-known site of Champ Durand in the Vendée, which was the scene of the first extensive excavations of a French Late Neolithic enclosure. The excavations were directed by Roger Jousaumme from 1975–1985 and evidence was uncovered to indicate that this was a heavily defended Late Neolithic causewayed enclosure (also known as 'interrupted ditch enclosures'). These enigmatic monuments are a characteristic feature of the Neolithic of western and northern Europe and comprise one or more discontinuous circuits of ditch with inner bank that are pierced or 'interrupted' by gaps or 'causeways' of intact earth. Archaeologists are of the opinion that

separate work gangs or kin-groups came together to construct the enclosures, with each one digging their own section of ditch.

Repeated ploughing within the interior of the Champ Durand enclosure had removed any possible traces of Neolithic buildings, and thus it was
unclear whether there had been a permanent Neolithic settlement here.
However, evidence of Neolithic domestic activity (e.g. animal bones, pottery,
quern stones, and flint tools) suggests that one had once existed at the site.
Whatever had gone on inside the enclosure at Champ Durand, it consists of
an inner, middle, and outer ditch, with each concentric ditch shallower than
the one that preceded it. There is also a single ditch closing off the southern
side of the site. In total, the ditches measure an impressive 2 km in length,
and the inner rock-cut ditch, which is the deepest of the three, measures a
substantial 5–7 m in width and c. 2.5 m deep. The excavation of one of the
entrances in the inner ditch (Interruption 77) uncovered the remains of a
hefty timber gate flanked by well-built dry-stone walls and probably also a
stone tower. Evidence for the latter came in the form of small animal bones
found at the base of the 'tower', which were probably the remains of owl
pellets. Roger Joussaume envisaged that in the manner of a medieval castle,
the Champ Durand enclosure had three defensive circuits, which got pro-
gressively larger as they moved inwards. If the site was being attacked, this
would have allowed the defenders on each rampart to fire over the heads
of those stationed on the one in front. Human burials (three double and
two single) were also found at Champ Durand, with all but one coming
from the middle ditch. More recently, Joussaume, has come to the conclusion that Champ Durand was originally a sacred enclosure, rather than a
defensive one. However, he is still of the opinion that at some point in its
later history, it was fortified against attack. Several archaeologists also agree
with this interpretation, even though it has become more fashionable to view
Champ Durand and the other Late Neolithic enclosures of western France
in a peaceful light.

The most common Neolithic enclosures in western France are the examples featuring the distinctive *pince de crabe* ('crab's pincers') entrances.
Basically, these entrances take the form of curving outworks that form an
additional outer entrance, although some *pince de crabe* enclosures could
be rather elaborate. For example, at the important site of Semussac, which
was excavated by Jean Pierre Mohen from 1966–1971, there were two *pince
de crabe* entrances and a complex series of outworks (Fig. 13). Although
ploughing of the site had destroyed any upstanding remains, many chalk
blocks found in the ditch fills hinted at the former existence of a substantial

rampart located between the ditches at the southern entrance. Possible evidence of a timber gateway was found here also.

Another important *pince de crab* enclosure is the site of Diconche, which lies about 25 km north-east of Semussac on a promontory that is flanked on one side by the valley of the River Charente. Excavations conducted here from 1987–1991 by Claude Burnez uncovered the remains of two successive Neolithic enclosures, with the outer and later enclosure featuring an elaborate *pince de crabe* entrance on its southern side (a more simple one was also located in the northern entrance). Post-hole arrangements found in the entrance indicated the former existence of timber gateways and perhaps also a narrow roofed tunnel. Chris Scarre has cast doubt on the idea that this evidence is defensive in nature, arguing instead that it 'suggests carefully controlled and probably tightly restricted access to the interior'.[5] Such ideas are plausible, but the idea that this entrance may have been fortified against attack should also not be simply rejected outright.

Interestingly, claw-like outer ramparts similar to those seen at French *pince de crabe* enclosures can be found at the entrances of some Iron Age hillforts; for example, those seen at the eastern entrance of the famous site of Danebury in Hampshire, which was investigated by Barry Cunliffe in one of the classic excavations of British archaeology. Huge caches of sling stones (some 11,000 round pebbles that were collected from four to six miles away) were found stored in a pit near this entrance at Danebury, and numerous sling stones were also found scattered around the passage that ran between the outer ramparts towards a timber gateway. It cannot be proven that these sling stones were hurled in anger during an attack on the site and that the ramparts functioned as fighting platforms. However, evidence for the burning of the gateway was also found in the eastern entrance, and this may well have been destroyed during an attack on the hillfort in the late first millennium BC. It is interesting to note that around the time of this attack, a new hillfort was built at Bury Hill some 6 km to the north of Danebury, perhaps representing the emergence of a new Iron Age polity that came into conflict with the one based at Danebury. During Cunliffe's investigation of the site, the skeletal remains of probable casualties of war were also found within some of the grain silos that had been dug in the interior of the hillfort by its Iron Age inhabitants. These remains comprised both complete and partial skeletons and many disarticulated body parts, several of which showed signs of extreme violence. For example, the skull of one man displayed three vicious blows, one of which had been caused by an iron spearhead, while a severe wound found on another male skull was probably caused by a sword, although it may not have immediately killed this individual; two sword cuts can also be seen on an individual's hip bone. Some of the isolated body parts could also have been war trophies, such as the decapitated skulls of two children found in pit 2509, that may have been displayed somewhere within the hillfort before they were buried.

Of course, this British Iron Age evidence does not prove that the French *pince de crabe* enclosures were also fortified sites. Indeed, it may be more probable, that a more circumspect reading of the archaeological evidence indicates that they were multi-phase sites, whose elaborate entrances were designed to impress rather than repel outsiders. However, we cannot completely discount a defensive role for the Late Neolithic enclosures of France, at least in some cases, and Chris Scarre's original thoughts on these sites should also still be considered even though such ideas are currently not in vogue:

'The scale of the defensive works suggests the existence of an authority capable of organising and directing their construction, and the appearance of such an authority may have been a direct response to inter-community stress and competition. The tension can be explained in terms of population pressure and the necessity to control critical but limited resources'.[6]

There are other possible Neolithic fortified sites found elsewhere in France, such as the enclosures built by the people of the NMB culture (Néolithique Moyen Bourgignon), which were often located on high ground and surrounded by stone ramparts and ditches that cut across promontories in the landscape. Such evidence is arguably indicative of a need for defence. In southern France, there are the enclosures of the Late Neolithic Fontbouisse culture, with one of the best known found at the site of Boussarges in Hérault. Here, the enclosure measured c. 30 x 45 m and was surrounded by a dry-stone wall that incorporated six circular towers or bastions; the site was also located in prominent topographical position. Not all archaeologists agree that these southern French sites were defensive in nature, arguing that the walls of these enclosures do not appear to have been built to any great height, and, that the so-called 'towers' or 'bastions' were actually shepherds huts or storage areas. Perhaps, but such arguments tend to ignore the fact that many of the Fontbouisse enclosures were built in naturally defensive positions in the landscape.

Italy

The Neolithic ditched enclosures of the Tavoliere Plain in northern Puglia, south-east Italy have been central to the story of the Italian Neolithic (and indeed, that of the wider European Neolithic), ever since they were first identified by British reconnaissance pilots during World War II (some 1000 enclosures are now known). Subsequent archaeological investigations carried out at some of these enclosures have uncovered evidence relating to the lives of early farming communities who lived in rectangular or trapezoidal wooden-framed wattle and daub houses, and who used a distinctive type of pottery known as Impressed or Cardial Ware (this pottery was a characteristic feature of the Neolithic of the western Mediterranean). It is probable that the first of these small ditched villages were built by settlers who had crossed the Adriatic Sea, perhaps from the Balkans. Several archaeologists have argued that at least some of the Tavoliere enclosures were fortified against attack. This is not unreasonable given that there are examples which had dry stone walls on the inner sides of their ditches and narrow funnel-like entrances that would have hindered access into their interiors. Furthermore, some enclosures were surrounded by as many as eight ditch circuits, with some ditches measuring a truly impressive 4 m deep and 6 m wide. It could even be possible that some of the earlier enclosures were fortified in response to the threat posed by hostile, indigenous hunter-gatherers. These groups may not have been willing to concede their lands to the incoming Neolithic migrants settling on the Tavoliere Plain, or alternatively, may have been sending out raiding parties to steal their livestock.

It may well be the case that there was no Mesolithic hostility directed towards incoming Neolithic groups who settled on the Tavoliere Plain (and indeed, there is little evidence for Mesolithic activity in the region), but evidence has been found at some of their ditched villages which reveals that it was not all sweetness and light between the first farming communities of Puglia. For example, at the site of Ripa Tetta, the skeleton of a young adult male was found lying in the enclosure ditch, and it was evident that his body had been scavenged by dogs/wolves soon after his death (suggesting he had been lying out on the surface). Another male found at the enclosure of Trasano has a large and fatal cranial fracture caused by blunt-force trauma. A female found at the site of Catignano I also displayed severe cranial trauma on her skull as a result of being clubbed in the head, although she appears to have survived due to the two 'trepanations' that she had undergone. It is interesting to note that some 3 per cent of Italian Neolithic skulls display evidence of trepanation, perhaps suggesting that many people received severe head wounds in episodes of violence and warfare.

Mention should perhaps also be made of the two Neolithic skeletons that were uncovered in the southern Italian town of Marsico Vetere in 2006, by construction workers digging a trench for the laying of an oil pipe-line. The skeletons dated to the late fifth/early fourth millennium BC and belonged to two individuals (perhaps a young man and woman) aged 20–25 years old. They were found with their limbs splayed out, suggesting that the dead bodies had been casually tossed into a grave. Analysis of their bones revealed that both individuals had suffered lethal skull fractures, and the Italian scientists who carried out this analysis hypothesised that the skull fractures indicated that the two individuals had been executed, or more spe-cifically, had been stoned to death. Perhaps then, they were criminals who had seriously transgressed against their community, and, as a result, paid the ultimate price. Or perhaps, they had been captured in an enemy raid and subsequently 'dispatched'?

Trepanned skulls have been noted on many other skulls from Neolithic Europe (and indeed on numerous skulls found at later archaeological sites around the world), such as the examples found in French Neolithic tombs by the previously mentioned Dr Prunières. These and other Neolithic skulls display large circular holes that were made with flint tools, and the roundels of bone that were removed in the process may possibly have served as charms or talismans in some cases. It is likely that some Neolithic trepanations were carried out to remove shattered fragments of bone, or to clean out blood that had pooled under the skulls of people who had been struck violently in the head with axes or wooden clubs, with this blood exerting painful and dangerous pressure on the brain. It could perhaps also be possible that some trepanations were 'exorcisms' performed on Neolithic people who suffered from mental diseases, and who were thus viewed as being possessed by malignant forces of some sort that needed to be released from their bodies.

The human remains found at Scaloria Cave, which is also located on the Tavoliere Plain, should also perhaps be mentioned here. Excavations car-ried out at this impressive cave-site in the 1930s and 1970s revealed that it was utilised by Early Neolithic communities c. 5500–5200 BC, and consists of an Upper and deep Lower Level, which is extremely difficult to access. Nonetheless, Neolithic people had made the tortuous descent into the lat-ter and deposited forty fine pottery vessels, which were found encrusted in stalactites. In the larger Upper Chamber, archaeologists discovered signs of seasonal habitation and the herding of animals, and evidence that the cave had also been used as burial site. Human bones from selected body parts (representing some twenty-five men, women, and children) were found scattered across the floor of the cave, mixed together with stone tools and broken pots. This archaeological deposit was somewhat similar to those found at previously mentioned Fontbrégoua Cave, and intriguingly as at the French cave, cut-marks from stone tools (mainly found on skulls, jaw-bones, long-bones, and clavicles) were also found on some of the human bones from Scaloria Cave. However, in contrast to the latter, there was no firm evidence to suggest butchery, nor was there any real indication to suggest that the individuals whose remains had been deposited in the cave, were the victims of a massacre (although one potential victim of violence was identified). Although we cannot totally rule out the latter, it is probably more likely that the human remains found at Scaloria Cave are related to the 'ritual defleshing' of the dead, similar to that already noted amongst the Aboriginal peoples of Australia. Whatever the truth, it appears that lower reaches of the cave were the focus of some sort of Neolithic cult.

Leaving aside ultimately unanswerable questions about the significance of the human remains at Scaloria Cave, Neolithic enclosed villages similar to those found on the Tavoliere Plain were built elsewhere in Italy, some of which have provided strong evidence for defence. For example, at the recently excavated site of Piano Vento in the Agrigento region of Sicily, a stone wall measuring c. 2.5 m wide extended for at least 400 m across most of the southern and western slopes of the hill on which the enclosure was built: in terms of defence, this was the most exposed part of the site. Inside the enclosure, archaeologists discovered the remains of circular and rectangular houses comprising stone foundations with wattle and daub walls. In the Vibrata Valley, northern Abruzzo (east-central Italy), there is the settlement of Ripoli, which was surrounded by a massive ditch measuring c. 5 m deep and c. 7 m wide. This ditch may well have been dug to express the status of the Neolithic community at Ripoli, as the many cattle bones, fine painted pottery, and the valuable imported goods that were found at the site, indicate that an important community which was socially prominent in the region lived here. However, while this is quite possible, the ditch could have had a dual purpose, also being dug as formidable defensive barrier that protected their wealth from enemy raiders.

Ötzi the Iceman: A Neolithic Casualty of War?

On 19 September 1991, two German tourists, Helmut and Erika Simon, stumbled across the frozen corpse of a man protruding out of a rocky ice-covered gully, whilst returning from a hike to the Similaun Mountain in the Ötzal Alps, which straddle the border between Austrian and

Italy. The authorities quickly arrived on the scene to recover the body, which proved to be a difficult three-day process, with some uncertainty as to which side of the border it lay (it was subsequently confirmed as lying just inside the Italian border). It was initially thought that the dead man was an unfortunate mountaineer who had lost his life in a modern climbing accident. However, nothing could be further from the truth, for the subsequent scientific investigation of his body (which continues to this day) showed that, remarkably, he was an inhabitant of Alpine Europe in the Late Neolithic c. 3200 BC, and was aged around forty-five years old when he died (a good age for the people of this time – measuring 5 ft 2 in he was also a small man). The 'Iceman' or 'Ötzi' (the nicknames by which this famous individual is now commonly known) undoubtedly represents one of the most important and extraordinary archaeological discoveries ever made. This prehistoric 'time traveller' from the Late Stone Age has provided unprecedented insights into a long-vanished world, that is, in many ways, still largely obscured from our sight.

An amazing and unparalleled collection of artefacts were found alongside the Iceman, including a small but finely made copper axe-head that was fixed into its forked yew shaft with birch tar and tightly secured with thin leather straps (Fig. 14), and a c. 2 m long yew bow with its accompanying quiver (made from Chamois hide). There were also fourteen arrow shafts, only two of which were fully finished and tipped with flint arrowheads. These were fixed to the shafts with birch tar and bound with thread, and also featured the remains of feather fletching at their ends, which would have helped to stabilise the arrows in flight. Ötzi also carried a small triangular flint dagger set into an ash-wood handle, that was kept in a scabbard made from tree bast, and also a 'retoucher' (a 12 inch long pencil-like tool made from a lime branch used for making flint tools), which he had probably employed in the production of his arrowheads and dagger. A 2 metre-long U-shaped, curved hazel rod, two narrow boards made from larch, and many pieces of hide found alongside his body, probably representing the remains of a backpack that he had carried high into the mountains.

Also found during the excavation of Ötzi's final resting place were the remains of his clothing, and it was evident that he had travelled into the mountains wearing leggings and a coat made from goat and sheep hide, with the latter reaching almost down to his knees. Also surviving were the remnants of one or two calfskin belts, and his shoes, which were made from deerskin and netting made from lime tree bast. Somewhat remarkably, Ötzi's right shoe was found still on his foot. Perhaps the best-preserved and most poignant item of Ötzi's clothing was his bear-skin cap, which had been held in place with a chin strap. The remains of a woven grass mat made from Alpine swamp grass were also found, and although its exact function is unclear, Ötzi may have used it as rain shelter.

More esoteric items were found with Ötzi, such as the white stone disc made from marble sourced from the Dolomites, which was pierced through the middle and threaded with twisted strips of hide, or the two hide strips onto which two lumps of birch polypore fungus were threaded. Interestingly, this fungus is known to have antibiotic and styptic properties and has been used for medicinal purposes down into modern times. Also worthy of mention are the sixty-one tattoos forming groups of lines or crosses that cover Ötzi's skin (which are likely to be related to acupuncture that helped ease his aches and pains), and the analysis of his stomach contents, which revealed that he had eaten bread, meat and vegetables for his final meal. Analysis of pollen found in his stomach also indicated that during the last thirty hours of his life, Ötzi had initially been up near the tree-line in the mountains, but had then returned to lower-lying pasture lands. After this he had then climbed back up past the tree-line to the high mountain zone where he died.

Scientific 'isotopic' analysis of Ötzi's teeth and bones suggests that he probably lived in the upper Eisack, or lower Puster Valley in South Tyrol, before moving on to the Vinschgau Valley, where he spent his last years as an adult. What though, led Ötzi to his lonely death high up in the mountains far from his home? Initially, it was speculated that he was shepherd or a copper prospector who been caught in a fierce storm, losing his life as a result of hypothermia. However, somewhat astonishingly (given the intense scientific scrutiny of his body), ten years after the discovery of Ötzi's naturally preserved mummy, a darker truth emerged – it was not the elements that had killed him but rather one of his fellow men. In June 2001, Dr Paul Gostner, a radiologist at the General Regional Hospital in Bolzano, was examining a new set of X rays of Ötzi's chest cavity when he spotted a shadowy object of some sort near the left shoulder – it was a flint arrowhead that had somehow been missed on the thousands of CAT scans and X rays of Ötzi's body, by the radiologists Dieter Zur Nedden and William Murphy. After this exciting discovery, new CAT scans revealed the small unhealed wound in Ötzi's shoulder blade, where the arrowhead had entered his body, showing that he had been shot from behind by his assailant. Computed Tomography (CT) analysis of the wound revealed that the arrowhead lacerated the left subclavian artery, and very probably caused almost immediate death through

major blood loss and shock-related cardiac arrest. Further evidence pointing towards violence was found on Ötzi's body and equipment by a team
of researchers led by Thomas Loy from the University of Queensland,
Brisbane. This comprised a deep knife cut on Ötzi's right hand and wrist
(said to have been inflicted shortly before his death), bruises on his body,
and most intriguing of all, traces of blood from four different people on his
equipment and clothing.

The big question, though, is what were the circumstances that led to
Ötzi's violent death? Here, we can only enter the realms of speculation, with
various imaginative scenarios put forward in this regard: Ötzi was ambushed,
but fought off his attackers who were attempting to steal his valuable copper
axe; he was a ritual sacrifice; or he was an important chief or shaman who
had been buried high up in the mountains (possible evidence for a modified
stone platform on which Ötzi may have been placed, was found near his
body). Taken as a whole, however, the archaeological and forensic evidence
that has been gathered from this diminutive, but hugely fascinating, Late
Neolithic individual, suggests that the most popular scenario for his death is
probably the most plausible one – Ötzi was mortally wounded in a battle or
skirmish with a rival group. This may have been sparked by a boundary dis-
pute, as Loy has speculated, but there could have been many other reasons
why Ötzi was drawn into combat with his enemies.

Iconographic Evidence

In addition to the above evidence for Neolithic Italian warfare, there are the
Late Neolithic north Italian 'warrior' stelae or statue-menhirs, such as the
one discovered in the pretty fifteenth century church in the village of Laces,
which is located in the Vinschgau Valley, close to where Ötzi would have
lived. Uncovered by accident during restoration work at the church, the
stele had been intentionally hidden below the wooden top of the church's
altar. Although only the mid-section of this recycled statue-menhir has survived, carved wavy lines (probably a belt) and clusters of dots and concentric
circles can still be seen on its surface, as well as a carving of a long-handled
axe, which can be seen on the top left of the stele in the chest area. This axe
is very similar in appearance to the one found with the Iceman, although
he would have been long-dead by the time the stele found in the church at
Laces was carved and erected. However he might have been familiar with
similar carved and painted wooden statues that perhaps preceded the stone
statue-menhirs.

There are also the stelae discovered at the site of Saint-Martin-de-Corléans, on the outskirts of the city of Aosta. During the second phase of activity (c. 2750–2400 BC) at the site, which was a centre of funerary and ritual activity from the Late Neolithic to the Early Bronze Age c. 3000–1900 BC, forty-seven anthropomorphic stelae resembling those found at the previously mentioned Swiss site of Petit-Chasseur were erected. As V. Rubinetto et al. have noted, the similarities seen between the Petit-Chasseur and Saint-Martin-de-Corléans menhirs points to cultural exchanges over the Alps during the Late Neolithic.[7] As on the famous Petit-Chasseur, and other North Italian Late Neolithic stelae, the figure seen on the Saint-Martin-de-Corléans example (Stele 30) has a schematic face comprising a simple brow line and broad nose, carries a bow across its chest, and wears a patterned garment of some sort. Just above the bow to the left, a hafted axe is also depicted, and a pouch can be seen hanging from a belt on the figure's waist, above which can be seen its clasped hands. A particularly impressive example of one of these statue-menhirs was found during a construction project in the town of Arco near Lake Garda: it measures over 6 ft tall, some 3 ft wide, and is nearly a foot thick. A simple face comprising a single line depicting a pointed nose with two eyes is carved onto its upper surface, along with a beaded necklace, while below, on the chest, there is an impressive array of long handled copper axes and daggers; below these is a band of wavy lines that probably represents a belt possibly made from copper beads. These superb statue-menhirs may have represented real or mythological figures, but they have been seen by Andrew Sherrat as hinting at a shift 'from the female, 'mother goddess' representations of old Europe and the far west, to the new, male qualities associated with warrior values'.[8] As we saw in Chapter 3, these values may well have emerged at the end of the Late Neolithic with the emergence of the Corded Ware and Beaker Cultures.[9]

Chapter 5

The Iberian Peninsula

A fitting place to begin this discussion of the evidence for Neolithic warfare in Spain and Portugal would be with what is regarded by many archaeologists as the most impressive fortified settlement of Neolithic Europe – Los Millares – the type-site of the important Late Neolithic Millaran Culture (Fig. 15). The site is situated some 17 km north of the city of Almeria in Andalusia, near the coast of southern Spain, and this hugely important proto-urban settlement or prehistoric 'town' was discovered and first excavated by the mining engineers, the brothers Luis and Henri Siret, in the late nineteenth century. More recent excavations were conducted at Los Millares in the second half of the twentieth century by the University of Granada, and analysis of the huge corpus of archaeological material recovered from the site is ongoing (the settlement covers some 5 hectares, and many hundreds of people must have lived here at any one time). Many scholars view large Iberian Neolithic settlements such as Los Millares as evidence of the existence of leaders or elite groups who had gained power through the control and accumulation of surplus products. Such control and accumulation would probably have aroused envy and greed – two unsavoury human traits that have often been the cause of warfare down through the ages.

Several archaeologists have questioned the defensive nature of Los Millares, and other probable fortified Neolithic sites in the Iberian Peninsula. Alasdair Whittle, for example, has argued that they 'can be considered...as deliberate demarcations of space, as takings of place, as eye-catching statements of communal identity...they may be more to do with display and the formalisation of movement in chosen places'[1] Sarah Monks, however, has questioned the validity of such arguments: '[they do] not provide an adequate explanation for why these monuments took the form they did. Many of the structures are distinctly defensive in form, and cross-cultural parallels reveal similar features within other societies'.[2] She has also rightly noted that these Late Neolithic sites were often built in naturally defended locations in the landscape (e.g. on hills, above cliffs, ravines, and rivers) with wide-ranging views, and furthermore, that there is significant evidence for burning

at several sites, with some sites actually destroyed and subsequently abandoned because of serious fires. Some of these fires could of course been accidental, but others may well have been ones started by enemy raiding parties.
The architectural features of these sites (e.g. towers, complex entrances) also
suggests that they were designed to be defended by archers, an idea which is
strengthened by the finds of large numbers of arrowheads at some sites, and
also by the skeletal and iconographic evidence from the Iberian Peninsula.

A good example of a cross-cultural parallel to Los Millares, and other,
similar Iberian Late Neolithic settlements, is the Chinese Late Neolithic/
Bronze Age site of Sanzoudian in the Cheifeng region of north-eastern
China, which was built by people of the Lower Xiajiadian culture c. 2000 BC.
The site is located on a high ridge above the Yin River, and was the subject
of rescue excavations carried out in advance of the building of a new local
dam, which brought to light the very well-preserved remains of circular
stone houses with courtyards, paved roads, and other installations. By far
the most impressive aspect of the site, however, was the huge stone wall
with semi-circular stone towers that ran across the south and south-western
part of the site, with an outer enclosure that was probably added at a later
in the Lower Xiajiadian (Fig. 16). This wall was actually constructed using
two parallel lines of large stone, and both the inner and outer wall measured
c. 6 m high by c. 4 m in width. The wall was built on the side of the site
where the terrain was relatively flat, in comparison to the steep river cliffs
that lay on the sites' northern and eastern sides, strongly suggesting that it
was defensive in nature. It has been argued that these impressive walls may
well have expressed communal identity and the power of local leaders, but
such concerns were secondary to their main role as fortifications.[3] Much
the same could be argued for Los Millares and of the other Late Neolithic
enclosed sites of the Iberian Peninsula that are being discussed here.

The builders of Los Millares (which was inhabited from c.3200–2300
BC) located their settlement on the highest point of a promontory at the
confluence of the River Andarax and the smaller Rambla de Huéchar. The
settlement is surrounded by steep scarps on all sides except the western one,
where there is a lower lying area containing an impressive megalithic cemetery of over eighty tombs (many of which are corbelled 'tholos' or 'beehive'
tombs not that dissimilar to the ones built by the famous Mycenaeans of Late
Bronze Age Greece). Many fine artefacts or 'prestige' goods (e.g. copper and
flint daggers, decorated stone plaques, bone 'idols', ivory and ostrich egg-
shell from North Africa) were recovered when these tombs were excavated.
The fact that they were not distributed evenly hints at the existence of social

stratification at Los Millares, with an elite ranked group perhaps in charge of those who were not afforded the privilege of burial in a megalithic tomb. The remains of many stone round houses that are typical of the Millaran culture were also found within the walls of Los Millares, some of which contained evidence of copper working. The remains of a metallurgical workshop, which contained a mass of metalworking debris and a furnace, was also discovered near one of the walls during excavations at the site in 1985.

It is with the fortifications that surrounded Los Millares that we are obviously primarily concerned, however. It has been estimated that the labour invested in their construction represents about 150,000 working days,[4] and although such estimates are of course, ultimately 'guestimates', there can be little doubt that much time and effort would have gone into the construction of the Los Millares fortifications. The construction of the three walls and associated features that comprise these fortifications, must also have surely been planned and overseen by skilled Neolithic 'engineers'.[5]

All of the walls at Los Millares were built using the local limestone and consist of double lines of large stones (held together with mortar) with an inner rubble core. In some places, the walls reach a very substantial c. 9 m in width, and there is evidence for their repair, reconstruction, and strengthening, with some of this work perhaps related to damage that occurred during attacks on the site. The second wall at Los Millares was built at the same time, or shortly after the inner one, but it is the outer and latest wall that is the most impressive. It measures over 300 m in length and incorporates several semi-circular and square towers, or bastions (at intervals of 11–15 m), and an elaborate barbican-like entrance which features a narrow entrance and narrow openings within its walls (measuring c. 12 m in length and c. 10 m wide, the 'barbican' was a substantial structure – Fig. 17). Why the builders of the barbican felt it necessary to incorporate narrow openings into its walls can never be known for sure, but their resemblance to the arrow slits that can be seen in many medieval castles is thought-provoking, and it can plausibly be argued that they were a defensive measure.

During the final phase of occupation at Los Millares, what have been interpreted as thirteen smaller forts, were built on the defensively exposed ridges surrounding the settlement, although only the best-preserved of these forts (Fort or 'Fortín' 1), many of which are in a poor state of preservation, has been fully excavated. The first phase of construction at the fort is represented by a central rectangular structure, which was surrounded by a bastioned wall and large ditch, while in the second phase, a further substantial ditch and wall with bastions was built around the inner wall (Fig. 18).

Not all of the Los Millares forts are of the same design as Fort 1, with some simply consisting of a large circular tower with a single narrow entrance and others taking the form of single enclosure walls with bastions. Some scholars disagree with the idea that these structures were actually forts, but they must surely have been built to provide visual coverage of the area surrounding the main settlement at Los Millares. This argument appears to be strengthened by the discovery of a small circular structure built just the south of Fort 1, which looks out over a part of the landscape that cannot be seen from the main settlement.

Another important Spanish settlement of the Iberian Late Neolithic is Valencia de la Concepción (Sevilla), which has yielded what may well be the remains of two unfortunate individuals who lost their lives in a failed attack on the site. Archaeologists found two skeletons in the ditch surrounding the site, and it was obvious from their position that they represented a hasty burial, with the dead accorded no special treatment and casually thrown into the ditch. One skeleton was also missing its head, while the other was missing a limb. This skeletal evidence coupled with the careless treatment of the bodies in death and the signs of burning that have been found at Valencia de la Concepción, perhaps more than hint that the settlement was subjected to a violent attack at some point. Further possible Neolithic casualties of war were discovered at the site of San Quirce del Valles (near Barcelona), where a circular pit containing two male skeletons was found. This pit seems to have been rapidly filled after the dead men were deposited in it, and their skulls had been subjected to crushing blows, either while the men were still alive or very soon after they had died.

Also perhaps worthy of consideration here, are the Late Neolithic ditched enclosures of the Meseta region of central Spain, which only came to light in 1999, as a result of aerial photographic surveys carried out in the region. Over fifty of these sites are now known, and although archaeological investigation of these enclosures has been mostly limited to 'ground truthing' (walking surveys that collect surface artefacts and identify any evidence for structural remains), three have been excavated: Gózques de Arriba, Fuente de la Mora, and Las Matillas, all of which are located in the lowlands of the middle Tagus basin.

Domestic evidence has been found at all three sites, weakening the argument that they were not inhabited by Late Neolithic communities, although it is former two that stand out in this respect. As well as the foundation trenches of circular stone houses, archaeologists working at the three sites discovered numerous pits that had been used to store harvested wheat and barley, many fragmented and complete grinding stones, and huge amounts of pottery: it was estimated that around nineteen tons would have been recovered from Gózques de Arriba if it was fully excavated, and some seventeen from Fuente de la Mora.

Hints that defence may have been of concern to their inhabitants have been found at both Gózques de Arriba and Fuente de la Mora. Although the former is located in a low-lying position, close to a tributary of the river Jarama, its inhabitants enclosed their site (c. 1 hectare in extent) with two ditches, with the outer one measuring some 3 m in depth. Fuente de la Mora was a similar sized settlement, and was located on a bluff above the Henares River. It features three enclosure ditches, with the interior one backed by a palisade, and these ditches had been dug on the north-eastern side of the bluff, the area which would have been most vulnerable to attack.

Late Neolithic settlements similar in design and plan to Los Millares have been found in Portugal, with the *Castros* of Zambujal, Vila Nova de São Pedro, and Leceia, in the Atlantic coastal region of Estremadura Province, the three major sites found here. João Luís Cardoso has pointed out that the location of these significant sites took advantage of natural defences (e.g. the tops of hills and scarps), that they were close to agriculturally fertile valleys, and that they also commanded natural routes through the landscape.[6]

Zambujal lies 10 km inland from the Estremadura coast, and was established at the beginning of the third millennium BC. Its builders located their settlement on an outlying flank or promontory of the Serra do Varatojo mountain range, which gave its inhabitants commanding views of the surrounding landscape. The site consists of a central 'citadel' with towers, which is fronted by a complex arrangement of outer walls and towers that run across the promontory. The walls are substantial constructions, ranging from c. 1.5–3.5 m in width and 3–7 m in height, and it is certainly of some interest to us that large numbers of flint arrowheads were found near the outermost wall.

Vila Nova de São Pedro, which is the type-site of the Late Neolithic 'Vilanovan culture', was located on a low hilltop, and consists of an inner thick-walled enclosure with external towers or bastions. Two outer arcs of walling with towers were attached to the inner enclosure. Hundreds of flint arrowheads were also found in caches at the site, suggesting that if they needed to, its inhabitants were well-equipped to defend their settlement from hostile forces. The presence of the arrowheads at both Vila Nova de São Pedro and Zambujal undermines the theory that these sites at least, were not defensive in nature, particularly when it is taken into account that hunting was no longer of any real importance to the Late Neolithic communities of Spain (and indeed those of the rest of Europe).

The site of Leceia, which is situated on a high, rocky plateau overlooking the fertile valley of the Barcarena River, began life around 3500 BC as a large, open-air settlement that may have been located here in order to protect the agricultural surplus produced by its community. After a period of abandonment that may have lasted as long as 150 years, people returned to the site c. 2800 BC, and three imposing circuits of wall (which covered an area measuring approximately 10,000 m²) with external towers were subsequently constructed. It is certainly of some interest that in one of the stone buildings at Leceia, the remains of three adult males were found mixed with domestic waste. It is not impossible that these individuals lost their lives when they attacked the settlement with a larger force, and were subsequently dumped or ritually buried in this building by its victorious defenders.

In addition to well-known sites such as Zambujal and Leceia, many smaller, Late Neolithic enclosed sites can be found in northern Portugal, such as those found in the Upper Eastern Algarve, with a noteworthy example, Cerro do Castelo de Santa Justa. The site was excavated from 1978–1985, and comprises a thick ellipse-shaped enclosure wall (c. 2–3 m in width) with ten towers or bastions. The earliest entrance at the site was a simple affair, consisting of two large stones side by side at the western end of the enclosure, which formed a funnel-shape; and these would have been closed by a wooden gate. This gate then became defunct when the site was later remodelled, and a larger and slightly more complex, L-shaped 'bayonet' gate was built projecting outwards from the eastern end of the wall. It is not implausible that the gates and towers at Cerro do Castelo de Santa represent succeeding defensive systems, and that the site was a fortified farming settlement.

In the Freixio de Numão region, there is the important site of Castelo Velho, which is located on a hilltop measuring c. 700 m in height, and which commands spectacular views of the surrounding landscape. The site basically consists of a large central tower inside an elliptical stone enclosure, with a larger outer wall surrounding this. The remains of several sub-circular structures can also be seen at the site, and during the archaeological investigations at Castelo Velho, an intriguing fragmentary deposit of human bones was found inside one of these buildings. This represented the remains of around ten individuals, with some bones displaying burning, cut marks, and evidence of gnawing by wild animals. Most of the body parts were missing, including skulls, and some have seen this skeletal evidence in the same light as that recovered from site of Leceia. Some archaeologists, however, have argued that rather than representing the remains of enemy dead, these bones are indicative of non-violent ritual practices carried out at Castelo Velho. This may well be the case, but a violent scenario is equally as plausible when it comes to interpreting these human remains.

Possible – if not probable – Late Neolithic fortified settlements are also known in the Atlentjo region of southern Portugal (e.g. Monte da Tumba, Porto das Carretas, Monte Novo dos Albardeiros). As with the other Iberian examples mentioned here, they were built on high ground with good visibility of the surrounding landscape, and were often located close to watercourses. They are also similar in design to other Portuguese and Spanish examples, comprising large central towers or 'citadels' that were surrounded by wide circuits of walls incorporating towers or bastions.

Skeletal Evidence from Spanish Neolithic Funerary Sites

In addition to the Beaker culture tombs of Costa de Can Martorell and Can Gol I and II, which were mentioned at the end of Chapter Three, there are other Neolithic funerary sites in the Iberian Peninsula that should be considered as places where victims of warfare may have been laid to rest. For instance, there is the cave-site of Lapa du Bugio, which is located in a sea-cliff on the Portuguese coast, some 40 km from Lisbon. Discovered in 1957, the subsequent excavations carried out at the site revealed its use as a Neolithic ossuary (c. 3600–2800 BC), with the remains of at least sixteen people (15 adults and 1 child) of unknown sex recovered from the slab-lined graves that had been dug into the floor of the cave. Re-examination of these bones in 1997, discovered an arrowhead embedded in the spine of one individual, which had entered his/her body from behind. There were no signs of healing showing that this individual had survived this injury, and he/she may have been trying to escape from an ambush when the arrowhead struck. None of the other of the individuals deposited in the cave appear to have died violently, although this does not necessarily mean that other victims of violence were not interred here.

Staying in Portugal, an individual of unknown sex from the collective burial at the Neolithic tomb or 'dolmen' of Ansião, in the mountainous area of the Alta Estremadura, was probably shot in the head with a flint arrow, with his/her assailant probably firing the arrow from behind and to the left. This archery attack is suggested by a small, triangular perforation seen on a skull fragment recovered from the tomb. However, in contrast to the individual from the cave of Lapa du Bugio, it seems that he/she had survived the attack, as there was evidence of healing and no sign of infection around this wound. Other skull fragments recovered from the tomb displayed healed, depressed skull fractures, which have also been noted on several skulls found at other Portuguese Neolithic funerary sites, as well as unhealed fractures that obviously led to death (e.g. at the caves of Algar do Bom Santo and Lugar do Canto).

Turning to the Spanish skeletal evidence, there are a number of Late Neolithic sites located in a small area of the Ebro Valley (the middle-upper area of the valley) of northern Spain that have yielded possible evidence of warfare, with the Longar rock-cut tomb or 'hypogeum' in the Navarre region providing some of the most suggestive evidence in this respect. Discovered in 1989 and subsequently excavated from 1991–1994, at least 112 people of all ages and sex were laid to rest in its burial chamber. Few artefacts accompanied the dead, but there were several leaf-shaped arrowheads inside the chamber, four of which were still embedded in the bones of the people that they had killed. It is very likely that the arrowheads which were not lodged in bones, were originally stuck in the long-since decayed bodies of the people they had killed.

The most notable of the sites in the Middle-Upper Ebro Valley is that of San Juan ante Portam Latinam (Ávila) – another small rock shelter. The site was discovered by accident in 1985 when a farm track was being widened by a bulldozer, with a rescue excavation, immediately – and quite literally – following in the tracks of this discovery. Two more extensive seasons of excavation were subsequently undertaken at the rock shelter in 1990–1991, which fully revealed a mass Late Neolithic grave dating to 3000 BC.

The skeletal remains of at least 338 people were found crammed together within the confines of the rock shelter, and of the 153 individuals whose sex could be determined, 70 per cent were males and 30 per cent females, with many children also represented in the burial assemblage (c. 37 per cent). It was clear from the position of the skeletons, the grave goods found with them, and from the radiocarbon dates obtained on their bones, that many people within the shelter had been buried at the same time as, or, within a short space of time of each other.

A limited collection of grave goods accompanied the dead, and included evidence of personal adornment in the form of a perforated deer canine, and perforated wild boar tusks, one of which was found lying on the chest of an adult male skeleton. A necklace made from over a hundred sea-shells (*Dentalium sp.*) was also found still in position around the neck of an infant skeleton. A rather sad discovery was the skull of a small dog also found in the rock shelter, with the cut marks on its remaining neck vertebrae clearly revealing that that the dog's head had been decapitated.

Sixty-one flint arrowheads, were also recovered from the rock shelter, thirteen of which were still lodged in the bones of the people who had been interred here. Some of these had clearly taken the lives of the people they had struck, such as the one that had entered the chest cavity of a young adult male. This would have caused lethal damage, with massive haemorrhaging in the chest cavity and the aorta and left lung lethally damaged. Another arrowhead was found between the ribs of a probable male juvenile, and no signs of healing were evident on his bones, while another young adult male had been killed by the arrowhead that was still stuck in his spinal column. Not all of the arrowheads had been the cause of death, and for instance, the one found embedded in the occipital bone (rear of the skull) of a young male was surrounded by new bone and tissue growth, indicating healing. A mature adult male had also clearly survived for some time after an arrowhead had struck and lodged firmly in his right radius bone (forearm), with dense new tissue growth forming around the wound (in fact, the wound had healed so well that it was impossible to remove the arrow). It is interesting to note that most of the arrow-wounds were found on young adult males, indicating that as is often the case in both non-state and state-driven warfare, it was usually young men who were involved in the Neolithic conflicts of the Upper Ebro Valley.

Other possible warfare-related trauma was noted on some of the skeletons from San Juan ante Portam Latinam, such as the five healed parry fractures seen on forcarm bones, which may reveal how individuals raised their arms in defence against armed attackers, or the four cases of trepanation that were also recorded on skulls. Mention has already been made in the previous chapter of how in some cases, Neolithic trepanning may have been carried out on individuals who had received severe head wounds in warfare. Also of some interest is the skull of a child which displays small perforations and complete destruction of the cortical tissue in both the external and internal surfaces of the skull. These holes seem to have been made with a punch of some sort, and must have caused the child considerable pain, although it is unclear what long-term effects they may have had.

It is also highly likely that the remaining arrowheads found in the rock-shelter were not grave goods, as many displayed impact fractures, and several were also located in contact with, or next to bones, strongly suggesting that they had formerly been lodged in the bodies of the deceased. The arrowheads consist of two main types: simple foliate, spear-shaped arrowheads, and tanged arrow-heads, with the tang on the latter aiding the attachment of the projectile point to the arrow shaft. Both types of arrowhead would have been deadly weapons of war, but the foliate examples in particular would have been the most effective, with some of these large arrowheads measuring c.6 centimetres in length and weighing in at c. 4 grams.

Jose Ignacio Vegas et al. have said in regard to the evidence from San Juan ante Portam Latinam: '[It] could be considered an atypical collective burial, where originally several individuals who had died violently were buried. Later, others belonging to the same group, affected by a demographic crisis, were buried in the same place. This crisis would have developed in a more or less short period'.[7] What this crisis may have been can never be known, but as Vegas et al. have also noted, in both prehistoric and historic times, these crises were sparked by three factors: famine, war, and epidemics. What caused the episode of warfare that is very probably revealed by the skeletal evidence recovered from the rock-shelter, can only ever be a matter of conjecture. However, it is quite possible, as Vegas et al. have further suggested, that Neolithic conflicts erupted in the Ebro Valley because a dense Neolithic population (indicated by the large numbers of megalithic tombs in the region) was fighting over the fertile land and other natural resources that the valley had in abundance.

I should also mention a rare discovery made at the site of La Peña de Marañón (Navarre), a small rock-shelter located on the left bank of the Ega River, which was fortuitously discovered in the early 1980s during gravel extraction work in area. The site yielded evidence ranging in date from the final stages of the Late Upper Palaeolithic to the Iron Age, but it was only in the Late Neolithic layer that evidence of burial was found during the rescue excavation subsequently carried out here. Along with a few grave goods (perhaps the most significant of which, was a leaf-shaped arrowhead) many human bones were recovered from this layer, many of them in a fragmented and burnt condition (representing at least twenty eight people). It was perhaps because of their condition that a highly unusual arrowhead injury was missed during the initial analysis of the bones from the rock-shelter, and was only later found during their re-examination in 2012. This took the form of a small fragment from a broken flint arrowhead, which was embedded in a foot bone (a lateral cuneiform) from the right foot of an adult male. It could be the case that arrow had entered the bone through the sole of the man's foot, and that he was either lying on his back or running away, with his leg raised, when he was shot. Alternatively, he may have been shot in the instep with the arrow, and it could also be possible that this man was the unlucky victim of a somewhat freakish hunting accident. However, when considered in light of the other evidence from the Ebro Valley also discussed here, it may be more probable that he was ambushed or was wounded in a battle or skirmish with an enemy force, although his flight from danger would probably been very painful if this was the case.

In addition to those found at the San Juan ante Portam Latinam rock-shelter, several other trepanned skulls have been recovered at Spanish Neolithic funerary sites. For example, there is the one belonging to an adult male buried at the important Bell-Beaker necropolis of Ciempozuelos (Madrid), which was excavated at the end of the nineteenth century by Don Antonio Vives, Commissioner of the Royal Academy of History. Scientific analysis of this skull has indicated that this individual may well have been the subject of two trepanations, surviving the first one for over a year, but dying soon after the second one was performed on his skull. At least four trepanations have also been identified on the skulls of Neolithic individuals found at the cave-site of Cova de la Pastora near Alicante on Spain's south-eastern coast. Two individuals (one male, and the other of unknown sex) aged c. 20–25 appear to have survived their trepanations, as does an older man aged 40–45 years of age. An adult of indeterminate sex aged between 20 and 40 years, however, had succumbed to his Stone Age cranial surgery, as there were no signs of bone-regrowth around the hole made in his skull. However, the relatively small size of the trepanations seen on these skulls, may indicate that they are related to some sort of initiation ritual. Alternatively, they could be a mark of prestige carried by select individuals, rather than evidence of surgical intervention carried out on individuals with violent head wounds. However, it could be argued that the latter is more plausible.

Images of Spanish Neolithic Warfare

We will finish this chapter with an examination of the remarkable iconographic evidence of Neolithic warfare that has been found in Spain. This prehistoric 'art' not only provides us with a unique pictorial record of armed conflict and other scenes of daily life from the time of Europe's first farmers, but also shows the weapon that they clearly favoured in combat – the longbow. This is not surprising in light of the fact that it was clearly a deadly killing weapon that was particularly suitable for long-range and surprise attacks, and which minimised the danger to those carrying out such attacks (of course those who were attacked could also start shooting back with their own bows). This rock art tradition is found in various rock-shelters located throughout inland regions of the Mediterranean basin (the Spanish Levant, eastern Spain) and comprises three distinct styles, perhaps representing different Neolithic cultural groups: the Macro Schematic style, the Schematic style, and the Levantine style. It is with the latter style that we are concerned, because it is here that we find exciting-warfare-related scenes. Some scholars maintain that the Levantine rock-art can be attributed to final hunter-gatherer communities, on the basis of hunting and gathering images that appear in this style. However, as Sarah Fairén-Jiménez has pointed out, the portrayal of objects (e.g. arrowheads, baskets made from esparto grass, and bracelets) in this rock-art, which are only found on Spanish Neolithic sites, argues against this. Motifs seen in the rock-art panels also resemble those found on the Cardial Impressed Ware pottery that is such a characteristic feature of the Early Neolithic in the Mediterranean and which may well have been introduced by Neolithic settlers from 'overseas'.

Included amongst this rock-art that speaks silently but strongly of warring Spanish Neolithic communities are battle scenes, such as the famous examples found at the rock-shelters of Les Dogues, Cueva Remegia, and Cingle de la Mola Remegia in the province of Castellón. These depict opposing lines of stylised and energetic groups of warriors who appear to be running at each other whilst shooting their arrows, with some warriors also probably engaged in tactical flanking movements (Fig. 19). Research undertaken by George Nash in 1997,[8] at four of the Castellón sites identified different types of warrior figures with stick figures composed from simple brush strokes the most common. As Nash notes, these figures are normally positioned within the thick of battle and he thus plausibly concludes that these are common soldiers or 'infantry'. The second largest group of figures were painted more carefully, and are depicted with large calf muscles and narrow waists, which exaggerates their legs and shoulders, giving them a more imposing and powerful appearance. These figures can be seen integrated with the 'infantry' on some of the rock-art panels, and may thus indicate that they were individuals who possessed superior rank and status. Some of the figures display an obvious part of the male body and the likelihood is that they represent warriors who went into battle naked, unlike the few individuals who seem to be wearing trousers of some type or 'pantaloons'. Finally, there are the more elaborately dressed warriors who can be seen wearing headdresses of some sort. These headdresses range in design from a simple blob seen above the heads of figures, to complex ones that may well have been made of feathers, and were perhaps somewhat similar to the famous war 'bonnets' worn by American Plains Indians when they went into battle. These figures are normally seen to the rear of the archery battles, and they may therefore represent war leaders of some sort who controlled and commanded their forces.

One of the best-known of all the images found in this Neolithic art, is the so-called 'phalanx' scene (in fact, this image was actually produced on a postage stamp issued by the Franco regime in 1967). This is found in the top-left hander corner of the battle scene at El Cingle de la Mola Remegia rock-shelter, and consists of five striding figures with outstretched arms, who are holding bows and arrows (Fig. 20). The figure leading the 'phalanx' wears some sort of tall headgear (or perhaps hairstyle) and this, coupled with his larger size in comparison to the other figures, suggests that again, we may be looking at a representation of a 'military commander'. There have been various interpretations of this phalanx scene, with some experts proposing that it may be a depiction of a war-dance performed previous to the battle, or warriors marching off to war. Others have suggested it may depict a victory 'parade' after the annihilation of an enemy group.

There are also images in the Levantine rock-art which take us much closer to the human suffering that goes hand in hand with warfare, wherever and whenever it was fought. The most moving of these images is also found at El Cingle de la Mola Remegia, and depicts a warrior (with his longbow above his head) carrying the body of his comrade who is probably dead, or dying, with the arms of the latter hanging limply from his shoulders (Fig. 21). In the same rock-shelter, there is also a scene depicting what seems to be an execution squad who, are walking away from their victim who lies on the ground in front of them with several arrows embedded in his body. The execution squad have their arms raised aloft, holding their bows in a triumphal and jubilant gesture. Of course, we have no way of knowing whether this scene portrays the death of an enemy or a 'criminal' who had carried out some serious wrongdoing, but the former is probably more likely. Another probable executed individual is depicted at El Cingle de la Mola Remegia, as well as what appears to be a wounded warrior wearing a probable feather headdress with two arrows stuck in his legs. There is a certain energy and dynamism seen in this running and stooping figure, and one can almost imagine his fear as he attempts to escape from and (unsuccessfully) dodge the arrows of his attackers (Fig. 22).

Who was fighting who in the Neolithic battles that are depicted in these remarkable and unique Spanish rock paintings can only ever be a matter of informed speculation. However, as in other areas of Neolithic

Spain and Europe, it is quite possible that they depict warriors from Early farming communities who were in conflict over land and other resources. Alternatively, they may possibly provide us with pictorial evidence of Early Neolithic incursions into Late Mesolithic territories, and the subsequent annihilation of the native hunter–gatherer groups who lived here.

Chapter 6

The British Isles

A
s in the rest of Europe, the British Isles have produced strong evidence for Neolithic warfare, with some of the most compelling coming from the three famous sites of Crickley Hill, Hambledon Hill, and Carn Brea. We will turn first to Crickley Hill, which is located some 4 miles south of Cheltenham on the Cotswold scarp. During Philip Dixon's later twentieth century excavations of the two-phase Iron Age hillfort on Crickley Hill, the remains of a Neolithic causewayed enclosure were also discovered (incidentally, there is strong evidence to suggest that the two phases of Iron Age settlement on the hill had ended violently, with evidence for burnt houses, gates, and slighted ramparts discovered).

The evidence recovered during Dixon's excavations on Crickley hill revealed an initial unenclosed phase of Neolithic activity at the site, with people digging pits and building small, temporary huts or shelters that may have been used by hunters or herders who stopped overnight on the hilltop. A small oval barrow also dates to this phase, although it contained no burial, perhaps suggesting that it had functioned as a cenotaph. After this ephemeral phase of occupation, Neolithic people settled on the hill and built a causewayed enclosure comprising two widely spaced ditches, which each had low but broad banks made from stone quarried from them, on their inner sides. Five entrances were identified in the outer ditch and at least three in the inner one, with a low fence or palisade (c. 2 m high) located to the rear of the former. This enclosure was then abandoned for some time after the deliberate slighting of its banks, with the dismantled material from these piled into the adjacent ditches. The bank material and the walls of the ditches also showed signs of having been burnt.

Following this abandonment, a new Neolithic community arrived on the hill and they enclosed their settlement with a single, but massive ditch, featuring two timber-lined gateways. Like its predecessors, this ditch was backed by a low broad stone bank or platform with low, inner fences or palisades (Fig. 23). However it was larger and more complicated in its construction and consisted of a complicated series of interlocking cells, reminiscent of a Cotswold-Severn cairn. As their name suggests, these distinctive chambered tombs are concentrated in south-west England, but examples can also be found in some parts of Wales. From the gateways of the new enclosure, a cobbled and fenced roadway led into its interior, where the foundations of rectangular timber houses were found along with evidence of the day-to-day lives of the settlement's inhabitants such as flint tools, pottery, and cattle bones. Also discovered within the second enclosure lay the remains of a small rectangular stone and timber structure, which the excavator interpreted as a ritual structure or 'shrine' used by the Neolithic settlement's inhabitants.

This second enclosure had clearly been attacked by a considerable force of archers, as over four hundred flint Neolithic leaf-shaped arrowheads were found not only in dense clusters in the two eastern entrances, but there was also a dense concentration of arrowheads along the line of the former palisade, and numerous examples were also found inside the enclosure itself (Fig. 24). It is hard to disagree with Roger Mercer's reading of this evidence: 'The enclosure seems to have been the target of intensive and tactically marshalled archery'.[1] It is also quite likely that this was no *ad hoc* raid but rather, that careful thought and planning had gone into its execution. Philip Dixon has suggested that the Neolithic people who made Crickley Hill their home, had such raids in mind when it came to building their causewayed enclosures: 'the ditches were presumably designed to break up and slow down an assault, and the low bank, or rather platform, would then serve as a killing ground, at point-blank range, against aggressors clambering out of the ditch'.[2]

It may be possible that some of the arrowheads found strewn across the site are related to an earlier attack on the first enclosure, with the people behind this attack perhaps responsible for the destruction of its banks. However, a recent ('Bayesian') radiocarbon dating programme has indicated that the 'Battle of Crickley Hill' probably took place one dark day in the distant past c. 3500 BC (it has also revealed that British and Irish causewayed enclosures were built in a relatively short period from the end of the thirty-eighth century BC to the end of the thirty-sixth century BC). The distribution of the arrowheads at the site also indicates that the force which attacked Crickley Hill, overran the second enclosure, and it also seems likely that fierce hand-to-hand fighting with clubs and axes took place as its inhabitants tried to defend their homes and lives. We should also bear in mind that the Neolithic arrowheads found during Dixon's excavations at Crickley Hill, undoubtedly only represent a fraction of the projectiles fired at the enclosure, as many more will have been picked up or lost in the intervening

5,500 years since the Neolithic assault on the site.[3] Dixon's excavations also revealed that the second (and final) phase of Neolithic settlement at Crickley Hill had ended in flames with all the houses, gateways, and fences burnt down. Somewhat remarkably, some of the arrowheads found at the site were still lodged in the burnt timbers of one of the enclosure's gateways. In a short video aired on the Smithsonian Channel, the narrator reports that at Crickley Hill 'scientists have found evidence of Britain's first major civil war'.[4] This is a rather over-dramatic statement, but there can be no doubt that Crickley Hill was the location of a fierce battle, which must have resulted in considerable numbers of people being killed on both sides. However, the fact that the settlement was destroyed by fire and then abandoned, indicates that the victors of this armed conflict was the raiding party that attacked the site, rather than its inhabitants. It thus seems likely that it was the latter who suffered the most casualties.

In 1980–1981, Timothy Darvill excavated another causewayed enclosure at Peak Camp, which is located only about 1 km south of Crickley Hill. The excavations revealed Neolithic settlement activity contemporary with that on Crickley Hill, with a substantial pottery assemblage, flint tools, cattle bones, human foot bones, part of a cat's jaw, a broken sandstone disc, and part of an unusual shale arc pendant of continental style (but probably made in Dorset) amongst the artefacts recovered from the section of ditch that was excavated. It is quite probable that the two sites at Crickley Hill and Peak Camp formed a single, large, inter-linked Neolithic complex. With this – and the Neolithic archery assault at Crickley Hill in mind – large numbers of leaf-shaped arrowheads were also included amongst the artefactual assemblage recovered from the ditch section at Peak Camp. Could it thus be possible that there was a two-pronged attack, with both the Crickley Hill and Peak Camp Neolithic settlements being assaulted at the same time?

Hambledon Hill

Located just to the west of Cranborne Chase in Dorset, Hambledon Hill is an impressive and imposing, trefoil-shaped hill overlooking both the Stour valley and the Vale of Blackmore (Fig. 25). It is also the site of one of the most important Neolithic enclosures in Europe, and was excavated on behalf of English Heritage by Roger Mercer and his team in eleven seasons running from 1974 to 1984. There is not space here to go into great detail on the complicated evidence uncovered as a result of Mercer's investigations. Basically, however, the remains of a vast Neolithic complex dating from c. 3600 BC were revealed. This comprised a main causewayed enclosure and three 'outworks' on the Stepleton, Shroton, and Hanford spurs of the hill, with a smaller causewayed enclosure located on the Stepleton spur, and three sets of cross-dykes to the north, south, and east of the main causewayed enclosure. In the second stage of the site's history, a huge box-rampart c. 2–4 m in width and 2–3 m in height (without any additional breastwork) and substantial outer causewayed ditch, was built around much of the hilltop (c. 60 hectares). In the third and final stage, a further two smaller ditches were added to the exterior of the main rampart, with a smaller box rampart also constructed to the rear of the inner ditch. This was a remarkable feat of Neolithic engineering, as the main rampart alone would have measured some 3000 m in length, and it has been esti-mated that about ten thousand huge oak posts would have been needed to complete its construction (not to mention the massive amount of chalk rubble that would have filled it, and the vast quantities of timber hurdling that reinforced it). A similar number of posts would have been needed for the construction of the outer rampart. Access through the rampart was provided by three, huge timber-lined gateways with counter-hung gates, and two sets of double-ditched 'cross-dykes' were also located to the south and east of the main causewayed enclosure. Roger Mercer has suggested that although the Hambledon outworks were built separately, they seem to have been part of a grander and long-term plan, the end goal of which was to enclose the hilltop with formidable defences.[5] As we will see below, however, evidence found at the Stepleton enclosure strongly implies that these defences ultimately failed to serve their purpose.

The finds from within the main causewayed enclosure on the crown of the hill and the smaller Stepleton enclosure on the southern spur of the hill, indicate that the two sites had different functions: the former a place of ceremony and ritual, and the latter, an actual settlement, perhaps where a high-status Neolithic group lived. For example, within the main enclo-sure, there were some eighty pits containing deliberate and carefully placed deposits of pottery and polished stone axes from Cornwall. Two continen-tal stone axes were also found in the plough soil within the enclosure, one made from jadeite and the other from nephrite. Numerous pits were also found within the Stepleton enclosure, and these contained probable domes-tic refuse including animal bones, broken flint tools and pottery, carbonised wheat and barley grains, a probable oven or kiln base, and uniquely in Neolithic Britain, a grape seed. Numerous post-holes within the enclosure also pointed to the presence of former buildings, although they were not clear enough to indicate what these structures had looked like in their original form. It also seems that the people who had lived within this enclosure had ate well, as bones from whole joints of meat were found here also.

The building of the ramparts around the Hambledon Hill Neolithic complex strongly suggests that a very real and dangerous threat had appeared on the Neolithic horizon in Dorset. This threat had clearly materialised at some point, as excavations at the Stepleton enclosure revealed that the inner rampart had not only been set on fire for some 200 m of its length but that people had died violently here (the archaeological investigation of the Shroton outwork revealed that here too, the rampart had been set on fire, with some 140 m of it burnt down). The well-preserved skeletons of two young men were found sealed below the collapsed chalk rubble of the rampart, and the fine quality leaf arrowhead found among the ribs of one man revealed he had been shot in the back. Below him, the bones of a small child were also discovered, and initially, it was thought that this young man had been trying to escape from an attack on the enclosure with the child when he was killed. However, given the fact that the child's skeleton was in a much more fragmentary and weathered condition than the young man's, and, produced an older radiocarbon date, it is now felt more likely that the juxtaposition of the two is more likely a coincidence (however, the original interpretation of this skeletal juxtaposition could still possibly be correct). The bones of other children were also found in the segment of ditch where the young man lay and the skeleton of a young man was also found in the furthest ditch of the Stepleton enclosure, again with a leaf arrowhead positioned between his ribs. The skeleton had been gnawed by rodents, suggesting that the man's body was left lying uncovered for some time before the ditch naturally silted up, and a further two skeletons were recovered from the enclosure (one on the edge of the outer ditch, the other in the top level of the main rampart ditch – both had been gnawed by wild animals, indicating that they also had lain on the surface for some time). Interestingly, some care seems to have been taken in the burial of a young man that was discovered in a pit grave on the northern side of the enclosure. He was buried in a crouched position below scorched chalk rubble from the collapsed rampart, with a broken pot and a quern-stone. The care taken in this burial thus perhaps indicates that this individual may have been a casualty from the enemy raiding party who attacked and destroyed the Stepleton enclosure.

Somewhat surprisingly perhaps, only a few arrowheads were found during the excavation of the Stepleton spur (in fact, in total, only forty-two arrowheads were recovered from the entire Neolithic complex on Hambledon Hill) but this may be because the fiercest fighting took place elsewhere on the hill. Faint traces of what appears to be a third causewayed enclosure were located on its northern spur, with much of it probably lost below the large and impressive hillfort that was built here later in the Iron Age. In the preliminary excavation report, Mercer suggested that it may have been here where the main enemy assault took place, with the evidence from the Stepleton enclosure perhaps representing an opening skirmish.[6] Future excavations may perhaps prove this was indeed the case, and Mercer also comes to the conclusion in the definitive excavation report (which is a superb piece or archaeological scholarship), that the Neolithic complex on Hambledon Hill was probably attacked at least twice by enemy forces. The recent dating programme mentioned above has provided support for this idea, as it indicates that the two arrowshot victims had died on different occasions.

Why the Neolithic complex at Hambledon Hill was attacked can only ever be a matter of conjecture, but it is perhaps possible that it was raided for cattle. Large Herds of Neolithic cattle ranging over the meadows of the Stour valley would have been vulnerable to cattle rustling, and thus in times of danger, Hambledon Hill may been used as a great cattle corral by the Neolithic people who depended upon this livestock. Alastair Oswald et al. have suggested that the gathering together of different groups at causewayed enclosures, some of whom may have brought livestock and exotic goods with them, could also have provoked raids or violent clashes.[7] They have also argued that the massive 'defences' at Hambledon Hill may have been architectural features that were not defensive in nature, but rather, represented barriers restricting access into these presumably special places, which were also designed to visually impress outsiders.[8] Perhaps, but the suspicion remains that these features were designed primarily to deter rather than impress outsiders, and were built as fortifications. Such defensive measures may have been an unfortunate necessity in a somewhat unstable part of Early Neolithic Britain, which was more prone to warfare than peace.

Carn Brea

Regarding Neolithic fortified sites in Britain and Ireland, along with causewayed enclosures, we should perhaps also consider here a related class of Neolithic monuments termed 'tor enclosures', which are found in Cornwall and Devon. Carn Brea is the best known of these monuments, and was excavated by Roger Mercer on behalf of the Cornwall Archaeological Society from 1970–1973. Although there had been much destruction at the site, due to the building of the medieval castle and the nineteenth century hunting lodge cum folly which replaced it, considerable evidence for the former existence of a Neolithic settlement was nevertheless discovered on the site's eastern summit. Here, in a small enclosure (measuring around 1 hectare in area) Neolithic people had cleared the rock-strewn summit of the hill to create a series of 'terraces' upon which they built timber houses, the traces of which survived in the form of scatters of post and stake-holes. Much occupational debris was found here, including numerous pieces of broken pottery, flint tools, and also several complete and fragmentary stone axes.

On the eastern side of the summit, the Neolithic inhabitants of the site also built an impressive stone wall around the enclosure (featuring massive blocks of granite sourced from the hilltop, with many weighing 2–3 tons or more), which was linked to huge natural boulders to form a very substantial barrier. In its original form, this wall would have stood well over 2 m high and c. 2 m wide, and was fronted by a ditch on its eastern side. Neolithic activity on the hill was not just confined to its eastern summit as excavations outside the eastern enclosure on the south-eastern slopes of the hill uncovered slight but further traces of Neolithic occupation, and also the remains of cultivated fields. Surrounding this area of the hill (c. 6 hectares) the remains of another massive stone wall can be seen and Mercer's excavations revealed that it had complex, barbican-like gateways and a ditch measuring some 1.5 m deep. This outer enclosure is similar in appearance to the one found on the eastern summit, and the Neolithic pottery and flints found in association with it revealed that it was contemporary with the former.

It may be possible, perhaps, that the massive stone walls which enclosed the Neolithic settlement at Carn Brea, had more to with signalling status and exclusion, rather than defence. Whatever the case, Mercer's excavations provided evidence that must surely point towards a very violent end for this early farming community. As well as widespread evidence for burning at the Neolithic 'village', its enclosure wall, which was found to be in a collapsed state when excavated, seems to have been deliberately slighted in antiquity, and a huge number of leaf-shaped arrowheads were recovered at the site (703 – the highest number yet recorded at a British Neolithic site). Given that only some 10 per cent of the settlement area was excavated, it is probable that many hundreds more remain to be found at the site (hundreds of arrowheads have also previously been recovered from the site during earlier excavations and as stray finds). Interestingly, at Site E in the south-western corner of the enclosure wall, which was probably the main entrance into the Neolithic settlement, there was also a dense concentration of arrowheads. Many of the arrowheads found at Carn Brea also displayed impact fractures at their tips and bases, showing that they had hit something solid (like a huge stone wall perhaps, or a person's body?). Thus when considered cumulatively, the evidence from the eastern summit provides strong support for the idea that the site was attacked by a large assault force, which included many archers. Of course, it may be the case that some of the arrowheads found at Carn Brea were made by its Neolithic occupants in preparation for the site's defence. Indeed, this may have been a necessity, as on the basis of the archaeological evidence found at the site (e.g. pottery from the Lizard Peninsula, Cornwall, and polished stone axes from Wessex), it appears that the Neolithic community of Carn Brea was of some status, and flourished as a result of its involvement in a wide-reaching exchange network. The exotic goods that the Carn Brea community had acquired may well have been the spark that ignited the attack on this Cornish Neolithic settlement. How many people died in the assault on the Carn Brea Neolithic settlement will never be known, as bone does not survive well in the acidic soil on the hill-top. However, as the settlement was abandoned following this violent event, the suspicion is that many of its inhabitants lost their lives. Nevertheless, it is possible that the enemy force which attacked the Neolithic settlement at Carn Brea did not have everything their own way either, as some of the arrowheads found at the site were probably fired from bows wielded in its defence (unless the people of Carn Brea were totally 'outgunned' in a surprise raid carried out by a very large raiding party).

As yet, no firm evidence for attack and destruction has been found at any of the other Neolithic tor enclosures, such as the likely examples at White Tor (Whittor) and Stowe's Pound. However, we should briefly consider the results of the small-scale excavation that Mercer also undertook at the site of Helman Tor, some 40 km from Carn Brea on the edge of Bodmin Moor. He discovered a site that bore striking parallels to Carn Brea, with a very similar massive boulder-built wall enclosing a settlement area of around 1 hectare, where people had constructed houses on some twenty occupation terraces. A similar range of Neolithic artefacts came from the site, and not only was there was a high proportion of leaf-shaped arrow-heads amongst the lithic assemblage, but a layer of burning was also identified at Helman Tor.

Neolithic stone built enclosures are also coming increasingly to light in other parts of Britain, with likely examples found on Carrock Fell, Cumbria, and Gardom's Edge in the Peak District; there is also the interesting Welsh site of Gwaenysgor. The site is located just inland from the North Welsh coast in the hills above Prestatyn, and was excavated by Thomas Glenn in the early twentieth century. The site is located on the summit of Bryn Llwyn (or 'King Charles's Bowling Green' as it is also known), which commands wide-ranging views, particularly in the direction of the coast. Glenn found considerable evidence relating to the lives of a long-lost Neolithic community (and also an Early Bronze Age barrow containing a cremation burial in a stone cist grave). This evidence included polished stone axe fragments, flint tools, sheep/goat bones, oyster-shells, 'pot-boilers' (stones used for heating water), part of a probable shale arm-ring, finely made flint arrow-heads, two 'lance-heads' (these artefacts are now referred to as 'laurel leaves' by archaeologists but they may possibly have been used as spearheads), and numerous sherds of plain Neolithic pottery. Also found were thousands of glacial pebbles piled in heaps, and these may well have been collected for use as sling-stones, as Glenn suggests in the excavation report.

Glenn also uncovered the remains of a series of large stone walls enclosing the site, although it is perhaps unlikely that the wall on the eastern side of summit actually reached c. 5 m wide in places, as he notes in the excavation report.[9] Whether the glacial pebbles were indeed sling stones is hard to say for certain, but Glenn was clearly (and not unreasonably) of the opinion that the walls were defensive in nature and that the Neolithic settlement was deliberately fortified against attack from the sea: 'They were armed with the bow, lance, sling, and axe, and their arrow-heads and lance-tips were leaf-shaped; they were also skilled military engineers, and fortified themselves against a foe expected from the coast'. Whether this foe actually ever turned up is unknown, but a burnt layer was found in association with various artefacts (e.g. pottery sherds, animal bones and flint arrowheads) in one corner of the settlement, and may have represented the remains of a burnt wooden dwelling. Of course, such evidence provides a rather flimsy case on which to build an argument for the attack and destruction of the Gwaenysgor settlement by a sea-borne raiding force who swept in from the North-Welsh coast. However, the location and enclosure walls of the site do arguably suggest that defence was a concern for its Neolithic inhabitants.

Evidence that is arguably indicative of warfare has also been found at other British causewayed enclosures, with one of the strongest candidates in this regard the Hembury enclosure in Devon. Located on the southern end of the Blackdown Hills, Hembury was excavated by Dorothy Liddell between 1930–1935, as part of her investigations into the impressive Iron Age hillfort that had long been a familiar feature in this part of the Devon countryside. At the southern end of the hillfort's interior, Liddell unearthed Neolithic occupation debris such as Neolithic pottery and polished flint axes in a series of ditches. On the hillfort's western side, near its main entrance, she found segments of a substantial causewayed ditch with inner bank, some parts of which were c. 5 m wide and c. 2 m deep.

A further discovery in the area of the hillfort entrance, was a burnt Neolithic timber structure, which Liddel referred to as the 'guard-house' (it is more likely to have been a timber-lined gateway), and a mass of burnt timber comprising carbonised oak, hazel and ash. Whole blocks of oak and stone were also recovered from all the excavated parts of the inner ditch. It seems likely that this burnt material represented the remains of some type of wooden framework that had reinforced the front of the bank. Part of a causewayed ditch with a low but broad inner bank was also located near the north-eastern entrance into the hillfort during the excavations in 1934–1945, and this contained similar burnt material. Evidence of burning does not of course, provide proof of armed conflict at Hembury, but it is interesting to note that at least 120 leaf-shaped arrowheads were found during the excavations (many of which were broken and had been calcined by fire) in an area where there had probably been a wooden gateway. Furthermore, a major concentration of arrow-heads was also apparently found by Liddel near the 'guard-house', perhaps representing a fierce archery assault near this probable entrance into the enclosure.

Further possible evidence for Neolithic hostilities has been found at the magnificent Maiden Castle Iron Age hillfort, Dorset. The hillfort was famously excavated by Sir Mortimer Wheeler in 1934–1937, and during the course of his archaeological investigation of the hillfort's interior, he discovered two separate circuits of ditch from a causewayed enclosure running across its eastern knoll. In 1985–1986, Niall Sharples undertook a new investigation of the hillfort on behalf of the former English Heritage (now known as Historic England). Both Wheeler and Sharples uncovered concentrations of leaf-shaped arrowheads at the enclosure, with some found in the inner ditch and others within the enclosure itself. Some of the arrowheads from the ditch were discovered in association with large amounts of burnt oak and scorched blocks of chalk rubble, pointing to the burning of a timber-reinforced bank or palisade. Also, many of the arrowheads found at the enclosure not only featured proximal and distal breakages, suggesting that they had been attached to arrows that had been shot and hit something, but microscopic analysis also revealed that they had been hafted when 'deposited' at the site. Leaf-shaped arrowheads with broken tips and bases have also been found at the four-ditched causewayed enclosure that was discovered in 2014 during excavations at Caerau Iron Age hillfort on the edge of Cardiff, by a team comprising archaeologists from Cardiff University and over 250 local volunteers. These arrows may have been fired in anger during a Neolithic assault on the enclosure, although it could also perhaps be possible that they were broken during hunting trips, and then simply tossed away into the enclosure ditches.

British Neolithic Tombs and the Evidence for Death by Archery

In addition to the two young men from Hambledon Hill, other individuals that were obviously killed by leaf-shaped arrowheads have been found in some British Neolithic tombs. Although they represent only a handful of people it is worth reiterating that not all arrowheads would lodge in the skeletons of the Neolithic people they killed. In fact, leaf-shaped arrowheads are the most commonly found artefact in British Neolithic tombs, with other grave goods generally lacking, and thus it could be reasonably argued that it is probable that these were more often than not, instruments of death rather than 'votive' deposits (Fig. 27). In fact, it may be the case, that being killed in battle was one of the criteria for inclusion in a Neolithic tomb, which obviously only contained a small and privileged section of the early farming communities who constructed them.

The robust young 'man' (it may perhaps be possible that this individual was female) found in the southernmost chamber at the Ascott-under-Wychwood Cotswold-Severn tomb near Oxford probably died after being shot by a leaf arrowhead, as the tip of one was found embedded in his third lumbar vertebrae. Don Benson has made the intriguing suggestion that as the arrow seems to have been fired upwards, then the man could possibly have been mounted on a horse when he was shot.[10] Horse bones have been recovered from some British Neolithic tombs and causewayed enclosures, although these probably belonged to wild rather than domesticated animals. Whether mounted or on foot when killed, the hinge fracture seen on the arrowhead could suggest that someone had unsuccessfully tried to save this individual after he had been shot. A leaf-shaped arrowhead was also found lying in a suggestive position beneath the ribs of an adult who had been laid to rest in another chamber nearby: another possible casualty of war perhaps, and maybe even someone killed alongside the man who had been shot in the spine?

At the more famous Wayland's Smithy tomb (another Cotswold-Severn monument), which lies above the Vale of the White Horse adjacent to the Ridgeway (a trackway running c. 145 km through Wiltshire and Oxfordshire, which originates in the Neolithic if not earlier), there is strong evidence for multiple death. The remains of fourteen individuals (eleven males, two females and a child) were recovered from the earlier oval barrow (Wayland's Smithy I) that preceded the impressive trapezoidal megalithic long mound (unsurprisingly, Wayland's Smithy II) that so impresses visitors today (Fig. 26). One of these individuals had a snapped arrowhead tip embedded in his pelvis. The arrowhead to which it had once belonged was actually found in close association with the pelvis, and it seems likely that the other broken arrow-heads found amongst the skeletal material had once been embedded in the soft tissue of people's bodies. The marks identified on the bones of two individuals had also been gnawed by dogs, revealing that they had been lying on the surface for some time before their bodies were deposited in the wooden mortuary chamber that was constructed below the barrow.

A recent Bayesian redating programme of Wayland's Smithy I indicates that this monument was only in use for a short space of time (1–35 years), and thus it may be possible that all of the individuals buried here died together at the same time. If so, the evidence for violent death and the scavenging of some of the bodies by dogs, may point towards the massacre of a small Neolithic community by an enemy war party, although the fact that no evidence for violent trauma was found on any of the other skeletons perhaps argues against this. However, the fact that females and children were under-represented in its mortuary deposit may suggest that most of them were taken into captivity after the men of this community were killed. We have already come across this 'gender imbalance' at the LBK massacre sites of Asparn-Scheltz and Schöneck-Killianstädten, where women and children may well have been taken captive after the massacre of the men of their communities.

Two skulls recovered from West Tump long barrow in Gloucestershire, display lethal wounds that were probably caused by arrowheads, and cut marks seen on the right collarbone of another individual found here, suggest decapitation. An arrowhead with a broken tip was also found inside the burial chamber, and it is likely that it was responsible for the death of one of the people buried in the barrow. The two individuals with the probable arrow wounds on their skulls may have been shot by arrows that had arcing trajectories (i.e. arrows that were first shot upwards into the air) as was famously seen at the battles of Crécy and Agincourt, where English and Welsh longbow-men literally rained down death on their French foes from their powerful longbows. Alternatively, they could have been shot from above by archers standing in some sort or elevated position (perhaps the fortified bank of a causewayed enclosure?). Exactly where these people lived when alive can never be known, but recent radiocarbon re-dating of the burials from West Tump has shown that the tomb is contemporary with the Crickley Hill and Peak Camp enclosures which are located less than 2 km away. Could it thus be possible is that some of the dead who lost their lives in the fierce fighting that took place at the Crickley Hill (and Peak Camp?) causewayed enclosure ended up being laid to rest in West Tump long barrow and perhaps other Neolithic tombs in the locality such as the Crippets/ Shurdlington, and Belas Knap long barrows (as we will see below, this latter tomb has yielded possible warfare victims)? Wherever the individuals from West Tump were killed, the arrow wounds (and other injuries) seen on Early Neolithic skeletons in Britain coincide with a floruit in tomb and enclosure building. Therefore, it may be that these monuments reveal a prehistoric society riven be dangerous stresses and tensions, with early farming communities building them in order to 'stake their claim' on desirable areas of land.

Moving westwards into Wales and the beautiful Black Mountains area of Powys, a young adult recovered from one of the chambers of the Penywyrlod long cairn was found to have a flint arrowhead tip embedded in a rib fragment. It has been concluded from its superficial penetration of the bone that the arrow to which it once belonged had been fired from a fair distance away, and had hit this individual on its downward trajectory as he/she tried to turn away from its lethal flight. It is thus quite possible that this individual had been running from 'trouble' when it struck home, although whether it caused their death is unclear.

Excavations at the chambered cairn of Tulloch of Assery B, which is located at the northern end of Loch Calder in Caithness, also provided evidence that it was not just in southern Britain that Neolithic people were attacking and killing each other with bows. Part of a broken arrowhead of uncertain type was found embedded in the lower vertebra of a 'fully grown adult', placed in the main burial chamber. If not the cause of death, this projectile fragment would certainly have led to paralysis.

Further skeletal evidence pointing towards warfare amongst 'Scottish' Neolithic communities was also recovered from the famous Isbister chambered cairn, or 'Tomb of the Eagles', as it is more commonly known. Located on South Ronaldsy in the Orkney Islands, this remarkable Orcadian

Neolithic tomb, was discovered by farmer Ronnie Simison in 1958, and his since yielded the largest and best preserved collection of bones from Neolithic Britain (some 16,000 bones from around 350 individuals). Also found in the tomb, and giving it its striking name, were the talons and bones of several white-tailed sea-eagles, which were probably ritually deposited here in the Copper Age/Early Bronze Age c.2500–2000 BC. Of more interest to us is that at least 20 per cent of the eighty-five skulls from the tomb display violent injuries, with some examples having been caved-in or even split in two, probably as a result of ferocious blows from stone axes.

Not all of the individuals found in British Neolithic tombs and settlements, who were killed by archers, need not have been casualties of war. For example, some may represent murder victims (although if so, such murders could have easily escalated into revenge warfare as has been widely documented in the ethnographic record), sacrificial victims, or even tragic accidents. However, they do provide indisputable evidence that people used bows in armed conflicts in Neolithic Britain. This was arguably their prime purpose, as evidence from British Neolithic settlement sites indicates that the hunting of wild animals was not particularly common amongst Britain's first farming communities.[11] In fact, nearly fifty years ago, Humphrey Case remarked in a brilliant article on the arrival of the Neolithic in Britain, that: 'Large Numbers of Arrowheads combined with small evidence for hunting suggests that warfare may have been a seasonal occupation of stably adjusted Neolithic communities in our islands.'[12]

Neolithic leaf-shaped arrowheads are a common find, but unsurprisingly, the same cannot be said for the wooden shafts to which they were once attached. Nonetheless, there have been some rather remarkable survivals such as the leaf-shaped arrowhead recovered from Blackhillock bog near Fyvie, Aberdeenshire, which was still attached to part of a shaft that had been made from Guelder Rose wood. It has also been estimated that some Neolithic arrow shafts could have been as much as a rather fearsome, 1 metre long.

We are very fortunate that a few Neolithic bows have remarkably survived from Neolithic Britain, and it is clear that the best-known of these – the Meare Heath bow from Somerset, which was discovered in 1961 during peat extraction on the Somerset Moors – would have been a very deadly weapon if used in warfare. Only one half or 'stave' of this yew bow survived along with part of the rounded handgrip, but as the stave and the remains of the central handgrip total c. 99 cm in length, it is thus possible to estimate that the bow would have measured c. 200 cm in length when complete

(Fig. 28). The remains of the transverse and diagonal and leather webbing that had probably strengthened the bow, can also still be seen on the stave along with part of the terminal notch to which the bowstring would have been fitted. A modern reconstruction of this Neolithic longbow concluded that it was accurate up to an impressive 90 m and actually fired arrows faster than the longbows used in Medieval warfare. It may be possible that the Meare Heath bow was used in Neolithic tribal conflicts that flared up over access to grazing lands for domestic livestock on the moors, but whatever its original purpose, it would certainly have been a highly effective weapon for killing people. Neolithic bows have also survived in other parts of Europe. For example, three bows (one of them remarkably complete) were found at the remarkable Neolithic settlement of La Draga, on the eastern shore of Lake Banyoles, Spain, which has yielded a wealth of superbly preserved evidence pertaining to the lives of the early farming families who lived here. The complete bow is rather small (c. 110 cm), although like the other bows, it is thought to have been used for hunting rather than warfare, for which there is some evidence at La Draga.

British Neolithic Cranial Trauma

We should also consider here the important study of cranial trauma on British Neolithic skulls, which is being conducted by Rick Schulting and Mick Wysocki.[13] This study has reassessed the injuries seen on the skulls recovered by earlier antiquarians and archaeologists from the long barrows and chambered tombs of southern and northern Britain, and has highlighted both healed and unhealed injuries. In the latter category is the striking injury seen on the skull of an adolescent (probably female) from the well-known Belas Knap long barrow, Gloucestershire. This individual had received a powerful and death-dealing blow to the right side the head, leaving a massive injury, and although the killing weapon can never be identified for sure, it is likely that it was either a stone axe or wooden club. An adult female from Belas Knap had also clearly died from a fierce blow to the top left-hand side of her skull, where a fairly large unhealed oval fracture can be seen. Similar injuries have been recorded on the Talheim skulls, which as we have seen, were very probably caused by the polished stone axes used by LBK farmers. Further examples of unhealed injuries include those seen on the front (and probably also the back) of a probable female skull from the Coldrum tomb, Kent, and on a skull recovered from an unknown Dorset long barrow. This displays a large and distinctive figure-of-eight shaped wound that is reminiscent of the low-angled 'key-hole' or 'gutter wounds' seen on modern gunshot victims. Two intriguing parallel cut marks can also be seen just behind the earhole of the Coldrum skull, and it is not beyond the bounds of possibility that the woman's ear was cut off and taken as trophy by the person who killed her. Larger trophies of war may also perhaps have been taken from some of the individuals buried in the Coldrum tomb as cut-marks were found near the tops of two individual thigh-bones, indicating the removal of legs. The researchers who studied these bones, were of the opinion, however, that these marks were not indicative of violent practice.

The skull of a teenage boy (c. 14 years old) found during excavations at Tulloch of Assery Tomb A (which was located alongside the previously mentioned Tulloch of Assery Tomb B in Caithness) displayed evidence which suggested that the boy had been clubbed violently in the head. This was not a clear-cut case of violence, however, as it could not be properly determined whether the skull had been damaged prior to or after the death of the teenager. However, the former is perhaps more likely, given the other evidence under discussion here.

Also worthy of mention is the skull of a young male ('Cranium J') that was found at the impressive site of Duggleby Howe, one of a handful of rare (and huge) Neolithic round barrows raised by Neolithic communities in East Yorkshire, and which was excavated in the summer of 1890 by the antiquarian J.R. Mortimer. The barrow had been built over a central grave shaft (c. 3 m deep) in which five adults and a young child had been buried (other burials and cremations had also successively been placed over these primary burials), and Cranium J was found lying at the feet of an older adult male in the grave shaft. Two, large perimortem injuries can be seen on the left and right parietals bones at the back of the skull and these were the result of two fierce blows which must have killed the young man on whose shoulders it once sat. Less certain is what Cranium J represents: could the young man have been a sacrificial victim who was murdered so that he could serve his master in the next life, or alternatively was the skull a curated war trophy? We will never know, but there can be little doubt that the young man's end was not a peaceful one.

Of course, it can be argued that 'bashed in skulls' do not provide proof of warfare and we could be looking at inter-personal violence in some cases. However, it still seems likely that at least some of these injuries are related to episodes of warfare in Neolithic Britain, and reveal unknown stories of violent death on unknown 'battlefields'. These battlefields may have been causewayed enclosures or other places in the Neolithic landscapes of Britain such as farming hamlets, which were raided by enemy war parties who – like their more modern counterparts in non-state (and 'civilised') societies – did not differentiate between men women and children when it came to killing.

Turning to the healed cranial injuries, these mostly take the form of small, single depressed fractures with rounded edges, and have been found at sites such as the Norton Bavant (Wiltshire) and Dinnington (Yorkshire) long barrows. However, a male skull found during Paul Ashbee's famous excavation of the Fussell's Lodge earthen long barrow near Salisbury uncovered a skull that intriguingly, features three of these fractures in a row. These healed fractures can be seen on both male and female skulls and in fact, represent the most common injury seen on British Neolithic skulls, although it is hard to say for sure exactly what caused them. They are also similar to the healed depressed fractures that as we saw in Chapter One, have been found on some Greek Neolithic skulls. Like their Greek counterparts, the British examples may represent wounds received in non-lethal ritual fights, or alternatively, some were perhaps caused by sling stones or even glancing blows from arrows or spears.

An analysis of 378 Neolithic skulls from Denmark and Sweden has also identified healed and unhealed lethal injuries (on both male and female skulls), with this analysis revealing a greater percentage of the former injuries, perhaps indicating that non-lethal encounters were the norm. However, it also worth noting that at the Danish site of Pormose, a Neolithic male skeleton was found with a large bone arrowhead still lodged in his skull (Fig. 29). This arrowhead had entered the man's head through his nose, and pierced the roof of his mouth, and another bone arrowhead was also found still stuck in the breastbone of this very unlucky individual. Such evidence perhaps warns us that we should be wary of taking the Scandinavian Neolithic cranial injuries as proof that some form of non-lethal ritualised fighting was the norm, and rather that warfare may have been more common amongst Sweden and Denmark's first farming communities than might be thought.

Neolithic Head-hunters in Britain?

Almost seventy years ago, Stuart Piggott wrote in his classic work, *The Neolithic Cultures of the British Isles*:

It is difficult to escape from the conclusion that the Windmill Hill folk [named after the famous causewayed enclosure in Wiltshire] in England, in common with their Continental relatives in the Western Neolithic, practised some form of cannibalism, utilitarian or ritual, while the abundance of skulls represented at [causewayed enclosures] may point to it sometimes at least taking the form of head-hunting.[14]

Jackie McKinley's recent analysis of the human remains from Hambledon Hill, may not have brought to light evidence of cannibalism, but it has revealed evidence to suggest that headhunting may well have been practiced by British Neolithic societies.[15] Fifteen skulls were recovered from the ditches of the Hambledon Hill Neolithic complex (with the majority carefully placed on ditch floors), three of which still had mandibles and some of the upper cervical vertebrae of the spinal column attached, revealing that they were deposited as fleshed heads. A complete skull with two of its uppermost cervical vertebrae still attached was also found during excavations at the Staines causewayed enclosure (in the outer ditch). It seems unlikely that loved ones or revered individuals had their heads chopped off so they could be placed in the ditches of causewayed enclosures. Thus perhaps a more plausible alternative, is that these heads were war trophies deposited in honour of the Neolithic deities who were believed to inhabit or visit these rather enigmatic monuments. It may also be possible that some of the skulls which had clearly entered ditches of causewayed enclosures (and other Neolithic sites) sometime after the decay of the bodies to which they were attached, were curated war trophies rather than ancestral tokens.

Ethnographic accounts reveal that the motives behind headhunting were complex and varied widely. However, it is clear that that the decapitation and taking of human heads in non-state societies carried considerable social and ritual significance. Of course, headhunting would not only have allowed warriors to display their fierceness, but it would also have been an effective way of terrorizing the enemy.

Examples of headhunting amongst non-state societies include that carried out by warriors of the Torajada of the Central Celebes, Indonesia, who took heads in combat or in specific headhunting raids. These decapitated heads were seen as vital for ensuring the general well-being of their communities, and the crops they depended on. Human heads were also needed for the consecration of Torajada temples and young men also took the heads of their enemies in order to prove their bravery. Amongst the Asmat people of the southern Netherlands of New Guinea, where head-hunting actually continued into the mid twentieth century, the practice was related to male puberty and sexual development, with decapitated enemy heads placed between the out-spread legs of young boys on the edge of manhood. The Asmat also believed that the fertility of their gardens would be promoted if they hung the decapitated heads of their enemies in them. Until fairly recently, the Jivaro Indians of Peru cut off the heads of their defeated enemies and turned them into trophies by shrinking them down to the size of oranges, and by attaching carrying cords through holes in the forehead. This was done in order to prevent the 'muisak' (avenging spirit) of the dead person from taking revenge on their killers, and as the muisak was believed to reside in the mouth, the lips of the deceased were either sewn or pinned together. In New Guinea, Marind-Anim warriors set out on annual head-hunting expeditions to take the heads of non-Marind Anim people who were viewed as sub-human and not 'real people' like the Marind-Anim them-selves. Thus, for the Marind-Anim, these expeditions were somewhat akin to actual hunts, although rather than wild game, it was humans who were the prey. The Mundurucu of Brazil also carried out headhunting expeditions against outsiders (some of whom lived several hundreds of miles away), who were also viewed as game animals to be hunted for sport.

The famous Nazca/Nasca culture (c. 100 BC–800 AD) of southern Peru also took trophy heads in battle as revealed by abundant images of head-taking on Nazca ceramics and textiles, and by spectacular archae-ological discoveries such as the cache of forty-eight decapitated skulls found at the site of Cerro Carapo in the Palpa Valley. Although the Nazca culture did not shrink the heads of the enemies, like the Jivaro, they did pin their lips together and drill holes through the foreheads of the deceased so that they could be carried or displayed. Depictions of trophy heads with plants growing out of their mouths, and sprouting beans or ears of corn in the form of trophy heads, are not uncommonly depicted in Nazca art. It thus seems likely that there was some sort of supernatural link between head-hunting and the fertility of the land in Nazca society. Similarly, the Naga hill tribes of north-east India cut off the heads of their enemies, but these were transformed into 'ancestors' whose role was to sustain the fertility of the people and the land. Closer to home, the famous Celts of central and Western Europe were renowned head-hunters, and several Classical authors provided accounts of Celtic headhunting. One of the most famous of these comes from the pen of the Greek historian, Diodorus Siculus (first century BC):

> They cut off the heads of enemies slain in battle and attach them to the necks of their horses...The bloodstained spoils they hand over to their attendants to carry off as booty...and they nail up these first fruits upon their houses...They embalm in cedar oil the heads of the most distinguished enemies, and preserve them carefully in a

chest and display with them with pride to strangers.

If Neolithic head-hunting in Europe was indeed a reality rather than a speculative idea, then it could be that its origins lay in the preceding Mesolithic
with Europe's final hunter-gatherer societies, as a few Mesolithic sites have
yielded evidence that is suggestive of this well-documented practice. The
most famous of these is Ofnet Cave in Bavaria, where two 'nests' of skulls
were discovered in 1908, one comprising six skulls, the other twenty-eight.
Most of the skulls belonged to women and children some of which displayed
lethal injuries that had probably been caused by stone axes. At Hohlenstein-
Stadel Cave, the decapitated skulls of a man, woman, and young child from
the Late Mesolithic were also found. All three of the skulls also featured
lethal wounds, indicating that they had been clubbed to death before having
their heads cut off. Jean Zammit and Jean Guilaine have wondered whether
is possible that the skulls found at these sites may represent war trophies
taken by Neolithic outsiders rather than evidence of Mesolithic violence/
headhunting?[16] More recently, at Kanaljorden in Sweden, archaeologists
discovered skulls from partially decomposed heads set on wooden stakes on
a low stone platform, which was submerged beneath a shallow pool close to
a Mesolithic hunter-gatherer settlement.

Causewayed enclosures are not the only Neolithic sites to have yielded evidence of decapitation. For instance, in the Chute 1 oval barrow in Wiltshire,
an intriguing group of skulls arranged in a circle was discovered, and one
of these still had three vertebrae attached to it. Also worthy of note is the
unexpected yet intriguing discovery made during the excavation of a medieval mill at Bridlington, Yorkshire. Here, the partially cremated remains of
a skull with an atlas vertebra still attached was found in a pit alongside a
Neolithic flint axe, which may well have been the implement that removed
the head of this individual from his/her shoulders.

Neolithic Warfare and Genocide in Ireland?

Whether headhunting was a feature of life in Neolithic Britain, is open to
debate, but the evidence seen in this chapter reveals that warfare was certainly not unknown and in fact, the archaeological evidence suggests that
– in the earlier part of the Neolithic at least – warfare was a fairly common
occurrence. It would be harder, however to make a similar statement in regard
to Ireland, as in contrast to Britain, evidence for Neolithic warfare is not
particularly evident, although this could be due to chance and the vagaries

of archaeological preservation. However, there have been some discoveries which indicate that relations were always not amicable between Ireland's first farming communities, such as the tip of a flint arrowhead found embedded in the right hip of an adult male interred within the famous Neolithic portal tomb at Poulnabrone, County Clare (Fig. 30). Two other individuals with healed skull fractures were also found in the tomb, one of whom also had a fractured rib, suggesting perhaps that all three individuals had been involved in armed conflict. Whether the man who had been shot in the hip had survived his injury is unclear.

At the site of Thornhill near Derry City, limited excavations have revealed a series of successive palisaded enclosures built during the Neolithic, and that one of the later enclosures was burnt down. Around twenty leaf-shaped arrowheads were also found during the excavations, some of which were associated with this episode of destruction. It seems likely that more arrowheads would be uncovered if a more extensive archaeological excavation was carried out at the site. It has also been suggested by John Waddell, that the two parallel ditches and inner palisade found at the Donegore Hill causewayed enclosure in County Antrim are defensive in nature (the only confirmed causewayed enclosure in Ireland).

Possible evidence of an attack on a lone Neolithic Irish farmstead (dating to c. 3700 BC) was found at Ballynagilly, County Tyrone, where the remains of a burnt, rectangular wooden house (measuring c. 6 x 6 m) were found in association with six leaf-shaped arrowheads, with three recovered from the interior of the house, and three from the exterior. It could perhaps be possible that these arrow were fired at this Neolithic dwelling by an enemy raiding party, who also set the house on fire, although they may simply have been left by its former occupants who abandoned the house after it had burnt down. Other examples of burnt Neolithic 'houses' (some of these structures may actually have been places dedicated to religious ceremonies and rituals) have been found in Britain, such as the two well-known and impressive timber halls or longhouses discovered at the sites of Balbridie and Claish in Scotland, or the ones previously mentioned at Dorstone Hill, Herefordshire. It may also be the case that some of these buildings were deliberately set on fire by enemy raiders, rather than being ritually or accidentally set ablaze by the groups responsible for their construction.

Finally, it may be worth considering the recent (but controversial) idea proposed by Alastair Moffat of Irelands DNA, a commercial company offering direct-to-consumer genetic tests exploring people's ancestry.[17] The first farming communities of Ireland are now known to have arrived in Kerry c.

4300 BC and the men of these communities – like their counterparts across Europe – carried the Y chromosome lineage of 'G' (recent tests carried out on 26 of 31 Neolithic male skeletons from Germany, France and Spain reveal that they belong to the G group). Intriguingly, however, only some 1.5 per cent of Ireland's men carry the G Marker today, and this has largely been replaced by the Y chromosome DNA marker known as R1b, which is now carried by around 84 per cent of Irish men (this represents the highest concentration of the R1b marker anywhere in Europe). The origins of the R1b marker have been cautiously dated to the middle of the third millennium BC, and Moffat has therefore hypothesised that the long-lived culture of the so-called 'G-Men' in Ireland, was wiped out by incoming continental groups of the Beaker culture from Iberia c. 2500 BC. It has to be said that this is an intriguing theory, given that the famous complex of copper mines at Ross Island, Killarney National Park, was very probably established by Beaker settlers from continental Europe in the middle of the third millennium BC. Not all are happy with such ideas, however, arguing that there is no archaeological proof that incoming Beaker groups waged a genocidal military campaign against Ireland's first farmers.

Whatever the truth is about Ireland's 'G-Men' and their demise, it is probable that further discoveries relating to Neolithic warfare in Britain (and perhaps also Ireland) will be made at some point in the future, and the same can be said for the rest of Europe. Some scholars may argue that the various sites, artefacts, and human remains discussed in this book do not represent evidence of 'true' or 'real' warfare, but however you interpret the archaeological material covered in this book, it certainly reveals that Neolithic Europe could be a very dangerous place to live at times. This material reveals that many communities of the New Stone Age in Europe were not just preoccupied with raising their crops and animals, or with building impressive monuments for their dead – sometimes they were more concerned with wiping each other out.

Notes

Introduction

1. *Leviathan* (full title – *Leviathan or the Matter, Forme and Power of a Common Wealth Ecclesiastical and Civil*) was published in 1651 at the end of the English Civil War.
2. Brothwell 2009, 25.
3. Vankilde 2015, 608.
4. e.g. see Alan Beyneix 2012, 221–22.
5. Helbling 2006, 115.
6. Lambert 2002, 209.
7. Lambert 2002, 209.
8. In Gat 1999, 568.
9. In Gat 1999, 567.
10. See Maschner and Reedy-Maschner 1988 for a review of the fascinating evidence relating to prehistoric warfare in this region.
11. In Bamforth 1994, 99. It may be interesting to note that Saukamapee also says: 'The great mischief of war then, was as now, by attacking and destroying small camps of 10 to 30 tents, which are obliged to separate for hunting.'
12. Milner 1999, 110.
13. Milner 2005.
14. Parker Pearson 2002.
15. Smith 2009, 19.
16. Lee 2007.
17. See Gat 2006, 97–110 for his excellent discussion on the 'Security Dilemma'.
18. Published in 1996.
19. Published in 1984.

Chapter 1: The Earliest Evidence for European Neolithic Warfare: Greece and the Balkans

1. Runnels et al. 2009.
2. Runnels et al. 2009.
3. Standen & Arriaza 2000.
4. Runnels et al. 2009.
5. Perlès 2001.
6. Runnels et al. 2009
7. Kokkinidou & Nikolaidou 2009, 90.
8. Keeley et al. 2007, 64.

9. Golitko and Keeley 2007, 337.
10. Andreou et al. 1996, 575.
11. Andreou et al. 1996, 575.
12. Gligor 2010, 237.

Chapter 2: Warfare in the *Linearbanderamik*/Linear Pottery Culture

1. Wahl and Trautmann 2012, 77.
2. Potter and Chuipka 2010, 517–518. See this article for other prehistoric sites in the American South-West that have provided further skeletal evidence for violence and warfare.
3. Teschler-Nicola 2012,
4. Keeley 2014.
5. Boulestin et al. 2009, 969.
6. Boulestin et al. 2009, 975.
7. Turner & Morris 1970.
8. Meyer et al. 2015.
9. Meyer et al. 2015.
10. Wahl & Trautmann 2012, 88.
11. Whittle 1996, 176.
12. Golitko & Keeley 2007.
13. Speilmann & Eder 1994.
14. Mellaart in Gat 2006, 172.
15. Pavuk 1991.

Chapter 3: Corded Ware and Bell Beaker Burials: Evidence of Warfare *and* Warrior Groups?

1. Heyd 2007, 327.
2. Balter 2015
3. Schulting 2015.
4. This may be suggested by the varying amounts and types of weapons found in male Beaker burials.
5. Vankilde 2006, 415.
6. Sherrat 1997, 192.
7. Westermann 2007.
8. Mercer 2009.
9. Fokkens et al. 2008.
10. This interesting idea was proposed by my undergraduate supervisor at the University of Liverpool, Dr Joan Taylor, a firm advocate of the idea that the Beaker phenomenon represented a distinct cultural group rather than an attractive 'package' of ideas and artefacts.
11. Turek 2015.
12. Redfern 2009.

13. Woodward et al. 2006.
14. Wallis 2014.
15. Miller et al. 1986
16. Osgood & Monks 2000.
17. Mercer 2009.
18. O'Flaherty 200
19. Christensen 2004, 137.
20. Westermann 2007.
21. Soriano et al. 2015.

Chapter 4: France and Italy

1. Veniamov 1984, 208.
2. Villa et al. 1986, 431.
3. Lukaschek 2000/2001, 23.
4. Pickering 1989.
5. Scarre 1998, 126.
6. Scarre 1984, 241.
7. Rubinetto et al. 2014.
8. Sherrat 1997, 2000.
9. It may be however, that warriors are more noticeable in the archaeological record during this time, on account of the more obvious weaponry that they carried. It is possible for example, that the male LBK burials featuring arrowheads and shaft hole axes are actually the graves of men whose role as warriors rather than farmers/hunters (or both), was being symbolised in death.

Chapter 5: The Iberian Peninsula

1. Whittle 1996, 338.
2. Monks 1997, 18.
3. Shelach et al. 2011, 22.
4. Monks 1997.
5. See Esquivel & Navas 2005 for more on the sophisticated building techniques employed by Neolithic 'engineers' at Los Millares.
6. Cardoso 2000, 44.
7. Ignacio Vegas et al. 2012, 301, who have also noted (*ibid.*) that 'In prehistoric times these demographic crises have been attributed to three causal agents; famine, war, and epidemics, factors which in the end are inter-related.
8. Nash 2005.

Chapter 6: The British Isles

1. Mercer 2009, 152.
2. Dixon 1989, 153.

3. Schulting 2013. This loss, or later retrieval of arrowheads, should also be considered at other British Neolithic sites that have provided evidence of archery attack.
4. 'Stonehenge Scientists Find Evidence of Britain's First Civil War'. http:www.smithsonianchannel.com/videos/stonehenge-scientists-find-evidence-of-britains-first-civil-war/33131
5. Mercer & Healey 2008.
6. Mercer 1990.
7. Oswald et al. 2001.
8. Oswald et al. 2001.
9. Glenn 1914
10. Benson & Whittle 2007.
11. The same can also be said for many Neolithic communities in the rest of Europe.
12. Case 1969, 171.
13. Schulting & Wysocki 2005.
14. Piggott 1954, 47.
15. McKinley in Mercer & Healey 2008.
16. Jean Zammit and Jean Guilaine
17. See Holden 2013.

Bibliography

Acs, P., Wilhalm, T. & Oeggl, K. 2005. Remains of grasses found with the Neolithic Iceman "Ötzi". *Vegetation History and Archaeobotany* 14, 198–206.

Adams, D. 1983. Why There Are So Few Women Warriors. *Behavior Science Research* 18, 196–212.

Aldhouse-Green, M. 2002. *Dying for the Gods: Human Sacrifice in Iron Age and Roman Europe*. Stroud, Tempus.

Andreou, S., Fotiadis, M. & Kotsakis, K. 1996. Review of Aegean Prehistory V: The Neolithic and Bronze Age of Northern Greece. *American Journal of Archaeology* 100, 537–597.

Anthony, D.W. 1990. Migration in Archaeology: The Baby and the Bathwater. *American Anthropologist* 92, 895–914.

Anthony, D.W. & Brown, D.R. 2011. The Secondary Products Revolution, Horse-Riding, and Mounted Warfare. *Journal of World Prehistory* 24, 131–160.

Ard, V. & Pillot, L (eds). 2016. *Giants in the Landscape: Monumentality and Territories in the European Neolithic: Proceedings of the XVII UISPP World Congress (1–7 September, Burgos, Spain) Vol. 3/Session A25d*. Oxford, Archaeopress.

Arias, P. 1999. The Origins of the Neolithic Along the Atlantic Coast of Continental Europe: A Survey. *Journal of World Prehistory* 13 403–464.

Arkush, E. & Stanish, C. 2005. Interpreting Conflict in the Ancient Andes. *Current Anthropology* 46, 3–28.

Armit, I. 2011. Violence and Society in the Deep Human Past. *British Journal of Criminology* 51, 499–517.

Armit, I., Knusel, C., Robb, J. & Schulting, R. (eds) 2006. Warfare and Violence in Prehistoric Europe: An Introduction. *Journal of Conflict Archaeology* 2, 1–11.

Axtell, J. & Sturtevant, W.C. 1980. The Unkindest Cut, or Who Invented Scalping. *The William and Mary Quarterly* 37, 451–472.

Ashbee, P. 1984. *The Earthen Long Barrow in Britain*. Norwich, J.M. Dent.

Atkinson, J.C. & Evans, J.G. 1978. Recent excavations at Stonehenge. Antiquity 52, 235–236.

Bahn, P. (ed.) 1998. Tombs, Graves and Mummies. London, Phoenix Illustrated.

Bahn, P. (ed.) 2002. *Written in Bones: How Human Remains Unlock the Secrets of the Dead*. Devon, David & Charles.

Bajnóczi, B., G. Schöll-Barna, G., N. Kalicz, Z. Siklósi, G.H. Hourmouziadis, F. Infantidis, A. Kyparissi-Apostolika, M. Pappa, R. Veropoulidou and C. Ziota. 2012. Tracing the source of Late Neolithic *Spondylus* shell ornaments by stable isotope chemistry and cathodoluminescense microscopy. *Journal of Archaeological Science* XXX, 1–9.

Balter, M. 2015. *Mysterious Indo-European homeland may have been in the steppes of Ukraine and Russia*. www.sciencemag.org/news/2015/02/mysterious-indo-european-homeland-may-have-been-steppes-ukraine-and-russia.

Bamforth, D.B. 1994. Indigenous People, Indigenous Violence: Precontact Violence on the North American Great Plains. *Man* 29, 95–115.

Barclay, G.J., Brophy, K. & MacGregor, G. 2002. A Neolithic Building at Claish Farm near Callendar, Stirling Council, Scotland UK. *Antiquity* 76, 23–24.

Barfield, L. 1994. The Iceman reviewed. *Antiquity* 68, 10–26.

Barfield, L. & Chippindale, C. 1997. Meaning in the Later Prehistoric Rock-Engravings of Mont Bego, Alpes-Maritimes, France. *Proceedings of the Prehistoric Society* 63, 103–128.

Bayliss, A., Whittle. A. & Wysocki, M. 2007. Talking About My Generation: the Date of the West Kennet Long Barrow. *Cambridge Archaeological Journal* 71, 85–101.

Bar-Yosef, O. 1986. The Walls of Jericho: An Alternative Interpretation. *Current Anthropology* 27, 157–162.

Benson, D. & Whittle, A. 2007. Building Memories: The Neolithic Cotswold Long Barrow at Ascott-Under-Wychwood, Oxfordshire. Oxford, Oxbow.

Bentley, R. A, Krause, R., Price, T.D. & Kaufmann, B. 2003. Human Mobilty at the Early Neolithic Settlement at Vaihingen, Germany: Evidence from Strontium Isotope Analysis. *Archaeometry* 45, 471–486.

Bentley, R.A., Wahl, J., Douglas-Price, T. & Atkinson, T.C. 2008. Isotopic signatures and hereditary traits: snapshot of a Neolithic community in Germany. *Antiquity* 82, 290–304.

Besse, M. 2004. Sion Petit Chasseur. In Bogucki, P. & Crabtree, P.J, Ancient Europe 8000 BC–AD 1000: *Encyclopedia of the Barbarian World. Volume 1: the Mesolithic to Copper Age (c.8000–2000 BC), 446–450*. New York, Thomson & Gale.

Beyneix, A. 2012. Neolithic violence in France: an overview. In Schulting, S. & Fibiger, L., *Sticks, Stones, and Broken Bones: Neolithic Violence in a European Perspective*, 207–222. Oxford, Oxford University Press.

Billman, B.R., Lambert, P.M. & Banks, L.L. 2000. Cannibalism, Warfare and Drought in the Mesa Verde region during the Twelfth Century A.D. *American Antiquity* 65, 147–178.

Bird, H. 1865. An Account of the Human Bones Found in the Round and Long Tumuli, Situated on the Cotswold Hills near Cheltenham. *Journal of the Anthropological Society of London* 3, 65–74.

Blanche, B. 1961. Early Bronze Age Colonists in Iberia. *Antiquity* 35, 192–202.

Blick, G. 1988. Genocidal Warfare in Tribal Societies as a Result of European-Induced Culture Conflict. *Man* (New Series) 23, 654–670.

Bogucki, P. 2001. Recent Research on early farming in central Europe. *Documenta Praehistorica* XXVIII, 85–97.

Borić, D. 2002. The Lepenski Vir conundrum: reninterpreation of the Mesolithic and Neolithic sequences in the Danube Gorges. *Antiquity* 76, 1026–1039.

Bostin, J.S. 2003. Blood Feud and Table Manners: A Neo-Hobbesian Approach to Jivaron Warfare. *Antroplogica* 99–100, 153–164.

Boulestin, B., Zeeb-Lanz, A., Jeunesse, C., Haack, F, Arbogast, R-M. & Denaire, A. 2009. Mass cannibalism in the Linear Pottery Culture at Herxheim (Palatinate, Germany). *Antiquity* 83, 968–982.

Brown, P. 1978. *Highland Peoples of New Guinea*. Cambridge, Cambridge University Press.

Brothwell, D. 2009. Biosocial and Bio-Archaeological Aspects of Conflict and Warfare. In Carman, J. & Harding, A. (eds), *Ancient Warfare: Archaeological Perspectives*, 25–38. Stroud, Sutton.

Brunwasser, M. 2013. Salt and the City. *Archaeology* 66, 35–39.

Burgess, C., Topping, P., Mordant, C. & Maddison, M (eds) 1988. *Enclosures and Defences in the Neolithic of western Europe* (i&ii). Oxford, British Archaeological Reports, International Series 403.

Burl, A. 1981. *Rites of the Gods*. London, J.M. Dent.

Carbonell, E, Caceres, I., Lozano, M., Saladie, P., Rosell, J., Lorenzo, C., Vallverdu, J., Huguet, R., Canals, A. & Bermudez de Castro, J-M. 2010. Cultural Cannibalism as a Paleoeconomic System in the European Lower Pleistocene. The Case of Level 6 of Gran Dolina (Sierra de Atapuerca, Burgos, Spain) *Current Anthropology* 51, 539–549.

Cardoso, J.L. 2000. The Fortified Site of Leceia (Oeiras) in the Context of the Chalcolithic in Portugese Estramadura. *Oxford Journal of Archaeology* 19, 37–55.

Cardoso, J.L. 2008 The chalcolithic fortified site of Leceia (Oerias, Portugal). *Verdolay* 11/Murcia, 49–66.

Carpenter, J. Archaeologists uncover a Neolithic massacre in early Europe. *Science*. [online] 17th August 2015. Available from: news.science.org/ archaeology/2015/08/archaeologists-uncover-neolithic-massacre-early-europe [accessed 5th January 2016].

Case, H. 1969. Neolithic Explanations. *Antiquity* XLIII, 176–186.

Chagnon, N.A. 1988. Life Histories, Blood Revenge and Warfare in a Tribal Population. *Science* 239, 985–992.

Chapman, J. 1994. Urbanism in Copper and Bronze Age Iberia? *Proceedings of the British Academy* 86, 29–46.

Chapman, J. 2009. The origins of warfare in the prehistory of Central and Eastern Europe. In Carman, J. & Harding. A. (eds), *Ancient Warfare: Archaeological Perspectives*, 101–142. Stroud, The History Press.

Chenal, F., Perrin, B., Barrand-Emam, H. & Boulestin, B. 2015. A farewell to arms: a deposit of human limbs and bodies at Bergheim, France, c. 4000 BC. *Antiquity* 89, 1313–1330.

Childe, V.G. 1958. *The Prehistory of European Society*. Middlesex, Penguin.

Christensen, J. 2004. Warfare in the European Neolithic. *Acta Archaeologia* 75, 129–156.

Clark, J.G.D. 1963. Neolithic Bows from Somerset, England. *Proceedings of the Prehistoric Society* XXIX, 50–98.

Clark, J.G.D. 1966. The Invasion Hypothesis in British Archacology. *Antiquity* XL, 172–189.

Conklin, B.A. 1995. Thus Are Our Bodies. Thus Was Our Custom: Mortuary Cannibalism in an Amazonian Society. *American Ethnologist* 22, 75–101.

Corcoran, J.X.W.P. 1964–1966. The excvation of three chambered cairns at Loch Calder, Caithness. *Proceedings of the Society of Antiquaries of Scotland* XCVIII, 1–75.

Cranstone, B.A.L. 1971. The Tilfamin: a 'Neolithic' people in New Guinea. *World Archaeology* 3, 132–14.

Cunliffe, B., Farrell. P. & Dee, M. 2015. A Happening at Danebury Hillfort – But When? *Oxford Journal of Archaeology* 34, 407–414.

Currant, A.P. Jacobi, R.M. & Stringer, C.B. 1989. Excavations at Gough's Cave, Somerset 1986–1987. *Antiquity* 63, 131–136.

Curwen, E.C. 1930. Neolithic Camps. *Antiquity* 4, 22–54.

De Donno, A., Santoro, V., Di Fazio, A., Corrado, S., Urso, D., Baldassarra, S. L., Di Nunno, N. & Introna, F. 2010. Analysis of Neolithic human remains discovered in southern Italy. *Journal of Archaeological Science* 37, 482–487.

Demoule, J-P. & Perlès, C. 1993. The Greek Neolithic: A New Review. *Journal of World Prehistory* 7, 355–416.

Diaz-Del-Rio, P. 2004. Copper Age Ditched Enclosures in Central Iberia. *Oxford Journal of Archaeology* 23, 107–121.

Dickson, J.H., Oeggl, K. & Handley, L.J. 2003. The Iceman Reconsidered. *Scientific American* 288, 70–79.

Divale, W.T. & Harris, M. 1976. Population, Warfare, and the Male Supremacist Complex. *American Anthropologist* 78, 521–538.

Dixon, P. 1988. The Neolithic Settlements on Crickley Hill. In Burgess, C., Topping, P, Mordant, C. & Maddison, M. (eds), *Enclosures and Defences in the Neolithic of Western Europe* (I), 75–89. Oxford, British Archaeological Reports, International Series 403.

Douglas-Price, T., Wahl, J. & Bentley, R.A. 2006. Isotopic Evidence for Mobility and Groups Organization Among Neolithic Farmers at Talhiem, Germany, 5000 BC. *European Journal of Archaeology* 9, 259–284.

Duering, A. & Wahl, J. 2014. A masscred village community? Agent-based modelling sheds new light on the demography of the Neolithic mass grave at Talheim. *Anthropologischer Anzeiger* 71, 447–468.

Edmonds, M. 1995. *Stone Tools and Society: Working Stone in Neolithic and Bronze Age Britain*. London, B.T. Batsford.

Ember, C.R. & Ember, M. 1992. Resource, Unpredictability, Mistrust, and War: A Cross-Cultural Study. *Journal of Coflict Resolution* 36, 242–262.

Esquivel, J.A. & Navas, E. 2005. The geometry and the metric used in the enclosure "Fortin 1" at Copper Age site of Los Millares (Almería, Andalusia). *Journal of Archaeological Science* 32, 1577–1586.

Fairen-Jimenez, S. 2007. Rock art and social life: Revisting the Neolithic Transition in Mediterranean Iberia. *Journal of Social Archaeology* 7, 123–143.

Ferguson, R.B. 1990. Blood of the Leviathan: Western Contact and Warfare in Amazonia. *American Ethnologist* 17, 237–257.

Ferguson, R.B. "The Causes and Origins of "Primitive Warfare": On Evolved Motivations for War." *Anthroplogical Quarterly* 73 (2000): 159–164.

Fernández-Crespo, T. 2016. An Arrowhead Injury in a Late Neolithic/ Early Chalcolithic Human Cuneiform from the Rockshelter of La Peña de Marañón (Navarre, Spain). *International Journal of Osteoarchaeology*, (wileyonlinelibrary.com) DOI: 10. 1002/0a.2513.

Fernández-Crespo, T. 2007. *Final Neolithic Mutiple Burials in the Upper Ebro Valley. The Case of San Juan Ante Portam Latinam (Basque Country, Spain)*. EEA Summer School eBook 1, 55–63.

Festi, D., Tecchiati, U., Steiner, H. & Oeggl, K. 2011. The Late Neolithic settlement of Latsch, Vinschgau, northern Italy: subsistence of a settlement contemporary with the Alpine Iceman, and located in his valley of origin. Vegetation History and Archaeobotany 20, 367–379.

Fibiger, L., Ahlstrom, T., Bennike, P. & Schulting, R.J. 2013. Patterns of Violence-Related Skull Trauma in Neolithic Southern Scandinavia. *American Journal of Physical Anthropology* 150, 190–202.

Fitzpatrick, A.P. 2013. *The Amesbury Archer and the Boscombe Bowmen: Bell Beaker burials at Boscombe Down, Wiltshire*. Salisbury, Wessex Archaeology.

Fokkens, H., Achterkamp, Y. & Kuijpers, M. 2008. Bracers or Bracelets? About the Functionality and Meaning of Bell-Beaker wrist-guards. *Proceedings of the Prehistoric Society* 74, 109–140.

Foreman, A. 2014. The Amazon Women: Is there Any Truth Behind the Myth? Www.smithsonianmag.com/history/amazon-women-thereany-truth-behind-myth-180950188/.

Fowler, L. 2002. *Iceman*. London, Pan.

Gat. A. "The Pattern of Fighting in Simple, Small-Scale Prestate Societies." *Journal of Anthroplogical Research* 55 (1999): 563–583.

Gat, A. 2000. The Human Motivational Complex: Evolutionary Theory and the Causes of Hunter-Gatherer Fighting, Part II. Proximate, Subordinate, and Derivative Causes. *Anthropological Quarterly* 73, 74–88.

Gat, A. 2006. *War In Human Civilization*. Oxford, Oxford University Press.

Gibson. A. 1994. Excavations at the Sarn-y-Bryn-caled Cursus Complex, Welshpool, Powys, and the timber circles of Great Britain and Ireland. *Proceedings of the Prehistoric Society* 60, 143–225.

Gilchrist, R. 2003. Introduction: Towards a Social Archaeology of Warfare. *World Archaeology* 35, 1–6.

Gleditsch, N.P. 1998. Armed conflict and The Environment: A Critique of the Literature. *Journal of Peace Research* 35, 381–400.

Glenn, T.A. 1914. Exploration of Neolithic Station near Gwaenysgor, Flintshire. *Archaeologia Cambrensis* XIV, 247–270.

Gligor, M. 2010. Funerary discoveries in Neolithic settlement from Alba Iulia – *Lumea* Novǎ (Romania): Multiple burial or ritual centre? *Transylvania Review* XIX (Supplement 5), 233–250.

Golitko, M. 2015. LBK Realpolitik: An Archaeometric Study of Conflict and Social Structure in the Belgian Early Neolithic. Oxford, Archaeopress.

Golitko, M. & Keeley, L. 2007. Beating plougshares back into swords: warfare in the Linearbandkeramik. *Antiquity* 81, 332–342.

Gonçalves, V.S., Sousa, A.C. & Costeira, C. 2013. Walls, Gates and Towers. Fortified Settlements in the South and Centre of Portugal: Some Notes about Violence and Walls in the 3rd Millennium BCE. *CPAG* 23, 35–97.

Groenman-van-Waateringe, W. 2011. The Iceman's last days – the testimony of *Ostrya cerpinfola*. *Antiquity* 85, 434–440.

Grygiel, R. & Bogucki, P.I. 1981. Early Neolithic Sites at Brześć Kujawski, Poland: Preliminary report on 1976–1979 Excavations. *Journal of Field Archaeology* 8, 9–27.

Gronenborn, D., Strien, H-C, Dietrich, S. & Sirocko, F. 2014. 'Adaptive Cycles' and climatic fluctuations: a case study from Linear Pottery Culture in western Central Europe. *Journal of Archaeological Science 51*, 73–83.

Guilaine, J. & Zammit, J. 2005. *The Origins of War: Violence in Prehistory.* Oxford, Blackwell.

Haak, W., Brandt, G., de Jong, H.N., Meyer, C., Ganslmeler, R., Heyd, V., Hawkesworth, C., Pike, A.W.G., Meller, H. & Alt, K.W. 2008. Ancient DNA Strontium isotopes and osteological analyses shed light on social and kinship organization of the Later Stone Age. *Proceedings of the National Academy of Sciences* 105, 18226–18231.

Haas, J. 1998. Warfare and the Evolution of Culture. *Santa Fe Institute Working Paper*, 1–35.

Haas, J. 1999. The Origins of War and Ethnic Violence. In Carman, J. & Harding, A. (eds), *Ancient Warfare: Archaeological Perspectives*, 11–24. Stroud, The History Press.

Halstead, P. 1993. Spondylus shell ornaments from late Neolithic Dimini, Greece: specialised manufcature or unequal accumulation?' *Antiquity* 67, 603–609.

Hallpike, C. 1977. *Bloodshed and Vengeance in the Papuan Mountains.* Oxford, Oxford University Press.

Harrison, R.J. 1980. *The Beaker Folk.* London, Thames & Hudson.

Harrison, P. 2008. The Pa Maori of New Zealand: The development of Maori fortifications after the introduction of firearms and artillery during the New Zealand wars of the 19th century. *Fort* 36, 5–21.

Hayden, B. 2003. *Shamans, Sorcererers and Saints: a prehistory of religion.* Washington D.C., Smithsonian Books.

Hayono, D.M. 1974. Marriage, Alliance and Warfare: A View from the New Guinea Highlands. *American Ethnologist* 1, 281–293.

Helbling, J. 1999. The Dynamics of War and Alliance Among the Yanoamami. *Sociologus* 49, 103–118.

Helbling, J. 2006, War and Peace in Societies without Central Power: Theories and Perspectives. In Otto, T., Thrane, H. & Vankilde, H. *Warfare and Society: Sociological and Social Anthropological Perspectives*, 113–141. Denmark, Aarhus University.

Heyd. V. 2007. Families, Prestige Goods, Warriors & Complex Societies: Beaker Groups of the 3rd Millennium cal BC Along the Middle Danube. *Proceedings of the Prehistoric Society* 73, 327–379.

Higham, T., Chapman, J., Slavchev, V., Gaydarska, B., Honch, N., Yordanov, Y. & Dimitrova, B. 2007. New perspectives on the Varna Cemetery (Bulgaria) – AMS dates and social implications. *Antiquity* 81, 640–654.

Holden, J. 2013. Is distinctive DNA marker proof of ancient genocide? Irish Times, http://www.irishtimes.com/news/science/is-distinctive-dna-marker-proof-of-ancient-genocide-1.1426197.

Hoogewerff, J. & Papesch, W. 2001. The Last Domicile of the Iceman from Hauslabjoch: A Geochemical Approach Using Sr, C and O Isotopes and Trace Element Signatures. *Journal of Archaeological Science* 28, 983–989.

Horn, C. 2013. Harm's Way: An Approach to Change and Continuity in Prehistoric Combat. *Current Swedish Archaeology* 21, 93–116.

Ivanova, M. 2007. Tells, Invasion Theories and Warfare in Fifth Millennium BC North-Eastern Bulgaria. In Pollard, T. & Banks, I. (eds), *War and Sacrifice: Studies in the Archaeology of Conflict*. Leiden/Boston, Brill.

Ives. S. 2003. Was Ancient Alpine "Iceman" Killed in Battle? *National Geographic News.* News.nationalgeographic.com/news/2003/10/1030_031030_icemandeath.html.

Jeunesse, C., Barrand-Emam, H., Denaire, A. & Chenal, F. 2014. Unusual funeral practices and violence in Early Neolithic Central Europe: new discoveries at the Mulhouse-Est Linearbandkeramik. *Antiquity* 342.

Jiménez-Jáimez, V. 2015. The Unsuspected Circles. On the Late Recognition of Southern Iberian Neolithic and Chalcolithic Ditched Enclosures. Proceedings of the Prehistoric Society 81, 179–198.

Jurmain, R. 2001. Paleopidemiological Patterns of Trauma in a Prehistoric Population from Central California. *American Journal of Physical Anthropology* 115, 13–23.

Kanter, J. 1999. Survival Cannibalism or Sociopolitical Intimidation?: Explaining Perimortem Mutilation in the American Southwest. *Human Nature* 10, 1–50.

Kaplan, S. July 8th, 2016. Grisly evidence of Neanderthal cannibalism uncovered in a Belgian cave. The Washington Post. https://www.washingtonpost.com/news/speaking-of-science/wp/2016/07/08/grisly-evidence-of-neanderthal-cannibalism-uncovered-in-a-belgian-cave/.

Keeley, L. *War Before Civilization*. New York/Oxford, 1996.

Keeley, L. 2014. War Before Civilization – 15 Years On. In Shackelford, T.K. & Hansen, D (eds). *The Evolution of Violence*. Springer, New York. DOI 10.10071978-1-4614-9314-3_2.

Keeley, L. & Cahen, D. 1989. Early Neolithic Forts and Villages in NE Belgium: A Preliminary Report. *Journal of Field Archaeology* 16, 157–176.

Keeley, L.H., Fontana, M. & Quick, R. 2007. Baffles and Bastions: The Universal Features of Fortifications. *Journal of Archaeological Research* 15, 55–95.

Kennedy, J.G. 1971. Ritual and Intergroup Murder: Comments on War, Primitive and Modern. In Walsh, M.N. (ed.). *War and the Human Race*, 41–61. London, Elsevier.

Kokkinidou, Dimitra and Marianna Nikolaidou. 2009. Neolithic Enclosures in Greek Macedonia: Violent and Non-Violent Aspects of Territorial Demarcation. In Carman, J. & Harding, A. (eds), *Ancient Warfare: Archaeological Perspectives*, 89–99. Stroud, The History Press.

Kotsakis, K. 1999. What Tells can Tell: Social Space and Settlement in the Greek Neolithic. In Halstead, P (ed.), *Neolithic Society in Greece*, 66–76. Sheffield, Sheffield Academic Press.

Knüsel, C. J., 2005. The Physical Evidence of Warfare – Subtle Stigmata? In Parker Pearson, M. & Thorpe, I.J.N (eds), *Warfare, Violence and Slavery in Prehistory*, 49–65. Oxford, Archaeopress.

Larick, R. 1986. Age Grading and Ethnicity in the Syle of Loikop (Samburu) Spears. *World Archaeology* 18, 269–283.

Lambert, P.M. 2002. The Archaeology of War: A North American Perspective. *Journal of Archaeological Research* 10, 207–241.

Larsen, C.S. 2015. Bioarchaeology: *Interpreting Behaviour from the Human Skeleton*. Cambridge, Cambridge University Press

Lawler, A. 2012. The Battle Over Violence. *Science* 336, 829–830.

Lee, W.E. 2007. Peace Chiefs and Blood Revenge: Patterns of Restraint in Native American Warfare, 1500–1800 *Journal of Military History* 71, 701–741.

Lillois, K.T. (ed.). 2011. *Comparative Archaeologies: The American Southwest (AD 900–1600) and the Iberian Peninsula (3000–1500 BC)*. Oxford & Oakville, Oxbow.

Loendorf, C., Simon, L., Dybowski, D., Woodson, M.K., Plumlee, R.S., Tiedens, S. & Withrow, M. 2015. Warfare and big game hunting: flaked-stone projectile points along the middle Gila River in Arizona. *Antiquity* 89, 940–953.

Lorkiewicz, W. 2011. Unusual Burial from an Early Neolithic Site of the Lengyel Culture in Central Poland: Punishment, Violence or Mortuary Behaviour? *International Journal of Osteoarchaeology* 21, 428–434.

Logue, P. 2003. Excavations at Thornhill, Co. Londonderry. In Armitt, I., Murphy, E., Nelis, E. & Simpson, D (eds), *Neolithic Settlement in Ireland and Western Britain*, 149–156. Oxford, Oxbow.

Loveday, R. 2002. Duggleby Howe Revisted. *Oxford Journal of Archaeology* 21, 135–146.

López-Montalvo, E. 2015. Violence in Neolithic Iberia: new readings of Levantine rock art. *Antiquity* 89, 309–327.

Lowell, J. 2007. Women and Men in Warfare and Migration: Implications of Gender Imbalance in the Grasshopper Region of Arizona. *American Antiquity* 72, 95–123.

Lozanova, A. 2014. Oldest City in Europe. Europost. www.eurpost.bg/article?id=11729.

Lukaschek, K. 2000/2001. *The History of Cannibalism*. Upublished Mphil thesis, University of Cambridge.

Lull, V., Micó, R., Rihuete-Herrada, R. & Risch, R. 2014. The La Bastide fortification: new light and new questions on Early Bronze Age societies in the western Mediterranean. *Antiquity* 88, 395–410.

Malone, C. 2003. The Italian Neolithic: A Synthesis of Research. *Journal of World Prehistory* 17, 235–312.

Maria Wild, E., Stadler, P., Haußer, A., Kutschera, W., Steier, P., Teschler-Nicola, M., Wahl, J. & Windl, H.J. 2004. Neolithic Massacres: Local Skirmishes or General Warfare in Europe? *Radiocarbon* 46, 377–385.

Marler, J. 1973. Warfare in the European Neolithic: Truth or Fiction? *Zeitschrifft für Archeologie* 7, 229–238.

Marquez, B., Gibaja, J.E., González, Ibáñez, J.J. & Palomo, A. 2015. *Projectile points as signs of violence in collective burials during the 4th and 3rd millennia cal. BC in the North-East of the Iberian peninsula.* In Marreiros, J. & Bicho, N. (eds), International Conference on Use-Wear Analysis 2012. Cambridge, Cambridge Scholars Publishing.

Marquez, B., Franciso, J., Gonzalez, J.E., Ibanez, J.J. & Palomo, A. 2009 Projectile points as signs of violence in collective burials during the 4th and 3rd millenia cal. BC in the North-East of the Iberian Peninsula. *Prehistoric Technology* 40, 321–325.

Márquez-Romero, J.E. & Jáimez, V.J. 2013. Monumental ditched enclosures in southern Iberia (fouth-third millennium BC). *Antiquity* 87, 447–460.

Maschner, H. & Reedy-Maschner, K.L.1988. Raid, Retreat, Defend (Repeat): The Archaeology and Etnohistory of Warfare on the North Pacific Rim. *Journal of Anthropological Research* 17, 19–51.

Mathew, S. & Boyd, R. 2011. Punishment sustains large-scale cooperation in prehistoric warfare. *Proceedings of the National Academy of Sciences* 108, 11375–11380.

McClure, S.B., Garciá, O., Roca de Togores, C., Culleton, B.J. & Kennet, D.J. 2011. Osteological and palaeoldietary investigation of burials from Cova de La Pastora, Alicante, Spain. *Journal of Archaeological Science* 38, 420–428.

Meggit, M. 1977. *Blood is their Argument: warfare among the Mae Enga tribesmen of the New Guinea highlands*. Mayfield, California.

Mercer, R. 1981. Excavations at Carn Brea, Illogan, Cornwall – a Neolithic Fortified Complex of the Third Millennium bc. *Cornish Archaeology* 20, 1–205.

Mercer, R. 1986. The Neolithic in Cornwall. *Cornish Archaeology* 25, 35–81.

Mercer, R. 1988. Hambledon Hill, Dorset, England. In Burgess, C., Topping, P., Mordant, C. & Maddison, C. (eds), *Enclosures and Defences in the Neolithic of Western Europe* (I), 89–107. Oxford, British Archaeological Reports, International Series 403.

Mercer, R. 1990. Causewayed Enclosures. Princes Risborough, Shire.

Mercer, R. 2009. The Origins of Warfare in the British Isles. In Carman, J. & Harding, A. (eds), *Ancient Warfare: Archaeological Perspectives*, 143–157. Stroud, Sutton.

Mercer, R. 2006. By Other Means? The Development of Warfare in the British Isles 3000–500 BC. In Armitt, I. Knüsel, C., Robb, J. & Schulting, R. (eds), *Journal of Conflict Archaeology* 2, 119–151.

Mercer. R. & Healey, F. 2008. *Hambledon Hill, Dorset, England. Excavation and Survey of a Neolithic monument complex and its surrounding landscape.* English Heritage Archaeological Reports.

Meyer, C., Brandt, G., Haak, W., Ganslmeier, R.A., Meller, H. & Alt, K.W. 2009. The Eulau eulogy: Bioarchaeological interpretation of lethal violence in Corded Ware multiple burials from Saxony-Anhalt, Germany. *Journal of Anthropological Science* 28, 412–423.

Meyer, C., Lohr, C., Gronenborn, D. & Alt, K.W. 2015. The massacre grave of Schöneck-Killianstädten reveals new insights into collective violence in Early Neolithic Central Europe. *Proceedings of the National Academy of Sciences* 112, 11217–11222.

Midgley, M.S., I. Pavlů, J. Rulf & M. Zápotocká. 1993. Fortified settlments or ceremonial sites: new evidence from Bylany, Czechoslovakia. *Antiquity* 67, 91–96.

Miller, R., McEwen, E. & Bergman, C. 1986. Experimental Approaches to Ancient Near Esatern Archery. *World Archaeology* 18, 178–195.

Milner, G.R. 1999. Warfare in Prehistoric and Early Historic Eastern North America. *Journal of Archaeological Resarch* 7, 105–148.

Milner, G.R. "Nineteenth-Century Arrow Wounds and Perceptions of Prehistoric Warfare." *American Antiquity* 70 (2005): 144–156.

Monks, S. 1997. Conflict and Competion in Spanish Prehistory: The Role of Warfare in Societal Development from the Late Fourth to Third Millennium BC. *Journal of Mediterranean Archaeology* 10, 3–32.

Nanoglou, S. 2001. Social and Monumental Space in Neolithic Thessaly. *European Journal of Archaeology* 4, 303–322.

Nash, G. 2005. Assessing rank and warfare-strategy in prehistoric hunter-gatherer society: a study of representational warrior figures in rock-art from the Spanish Levant, southeastern Spain. In Parker Pearson, M. & Thorpe, I.J.N (eds), *Warfare, Violence and Slavery in Prehistory*, 75–87. Oxford, Archaeopress.

Needham, S., Pitts, M., Heyd, V., Parker Pearson, M., Jay, M., Montgomery, J. & Sheridan, S. 2008. In the Copper Age. *British Archaeology* 101, 19–27.

Netting, R. McC. 1974. Kofyar Armed Conflict: Social Causes and Consequences. *Journal of Anthropological Research* 30, 139–163.

Newcomb, Jr, W.W. 1950. A Re-Examination of the Causes of Plains Warfare. *American Anthropologist* 52, 317–330.

Oeggl, K., Kofler, W., Schmidl, A., Dickson, J.H., Egarter, V.E. & Gaber, O. 2007. The reconstruction of the last itinerary of "Ötzi" the Neolithic Iceman, by pollen analyses from sequentially sampled gut extracts. *Quaternary Science Reviews* 26, 853–861.

O' Flaherty, R. 2007. A weapon of choice – experiments with a replica Irish Early Bronze Age halberd. *Antiquity* 81, 423–434.

O' Flaherty, R., Gilchrist, M.D. & Cowie, T. 2011. Ceremonial or Deadly Serious? New Insight into the function of Irish Early Bronze Age Halberds. In Ukelmann, M. & Modlinger, M (eds), Bronze Age Warfare: Manufacture and use of Weaponry, 1–14. Oxford, Archaeopress.

Osgood, R.Monks, S. & Toms, J. 2000. *Bronze Age Warfare*. Stroud, Sutton.

Orschiedt, J. & Haidle, M-N. 2013. Violence against the living, violence against the dead on the human remains from Herxheim, Germany. Evidence of a crisis and mass cannibalism?' In Schulting, R. & Fibiger, L. In Schulting, R. & Fibiger, L (eds), in *Sticks, Stones, and Broken Bones: Neolithic Violence in a European Perspective*, 121–138. Oxford, Oxford University Press.

Orschiedt, J., Häußer, A., Haidle, M.N., Alt, K.W., Buitrago-Tellez, C.H. 2003. Survival of a Multiple Skull Trauma: the Case of an Early Neolithic Individual from the LBK Enclosure at Herxheim (Southwest Germany). *International Journal of Osteoarchaeology* 13, 375–383.

Osgood, R. & Monks, S. 2000. *Bronze Age Warfare*. Gloucestershire, Sutton.

Ostendorf Smith, M. 2003. Beyond Palisades: The Nature and Frequency of Late Prehistoric Deliberate Violent Trauma in the Chickamauga Reservoir of East Tennessee. *American Journal of Physical Anthropology* 121, 303–318.

Oswald, A., Dyer, C. & Barber, M. 2001. *The Creation of Monuments: Neolithic Causewayed Enclosures in the British Isles*. Swindon, English Heritage.

Otterbein, K.F. 1968. Internal War: A Cross-Cultural Study. *American Anthropologist* 70, 277–289.

Otterbein, K.F. 2000. Killing of Captured Enemies: A Cross-cultural study. *Current Anthropology* 41, 439–443.

Otterbein, K. F. 2000. "A History of Research on Warfare in Anthropology." *American Anthropologist* 101, 794–805.

Otterbein, K. 2011. The Earliest Evidence for Warfare? A Comment on Carbonell et al. *Current Anthropology* 52, 439.

Otto, T. 2006. Warfare and Exchange in a Melanesian Society before Colonial Pacification: The Case of Maus, Papua New Guinea. In Otto, T., Thrane, H. & Vankilde, H. (eds), *Warfare and Society: Archaeological and Social Anthropological Perspectives*, 187–201. Denmark, Aarhus University Press.

Needham, S., Davis, M., Gwilt, A., Lodwick, M., Parkes, P. & Reavill, P. 2015. A Hafted Halberd Excavated at Trecastell, Powys: from Undercurrent to Uptake – the Emergence and Contexualisation of Halberds in Wales and North-West Europe. *Proceedings of the Prehistoric Society* 81, 1–41.

Pappa, M. 1999. The Neolithic Settlement of Makriyalos, Northern Greece: Preliminary Report on the 1993–1995 Excavations. *Journal of Field Archaeology* 26, 177–195.

Papathanasiou, A. 2001. *A Bioarchaeological Analysis of Neolithic Alepotrypa Cave, Greece*. Oxford, Archaeopress, BAR International Series 961. Oxford, Archaeopress.

Papathanasiou, A. "Health Status of the Neolithic Population of Alepotrypa Cave, Greece." *American Journal of Physical Anthropology* 126 (2005): 377–390.

Papathanassopoulous, G.A. (ed.). 1996. *Neolithic Culture in Greece*. Athens, Nicholas P. Goulandris Foundation Museum of Cycladic Art.

Parker Pearson, M. 2005. Warfare, violence and slavery in later prehistory: an introduction. In M. Parker Pearson & Thorpe, I.J.N (eds), *Warfare, Violence and Slavery in Prehistory*, 19–33. Oxford, British Archaeological Reports, International Series 1374.

Parkinson, W.A. & Duffy, P.R. 2007. Fortifications and Enclosures in European Prehistory: A Cross-Cultural Perspective. *Journal of Archaeological Research* 15, 97–141.

Pavuk, J. Lengyel-culture fortified settlements in Slovakia. *Antiquity* 65, 348–357.

Pertner, P., Gostner, P, Egarter, E.E., Rühli, F.J. 2007. Radiological proof for the Iceman's cause of death (ca. 5,300 BP). *Journal of Archaeological Science* 34, 1784–1786.

Pickering, M.P. 1989. Food for Thought: An Alternative to 'Cannibalism in the Neolithic'. *Australian Archaeology* 28, 35–39.

Piggot, S. 1954. *The Neolithic Cultures of the British Isles*. Cambridge, Cambridge University Press.

Piggot, S. 1971. Beaker Bows: A Suggestion. *Proceedings of the Prehistoric Society* 37, 80–94.

Pitts, M. 2014. Welsh hillfort hides rare neolithic enclosure. *British Archaeology* 139, 6.

Piqué, R., Palomo, A., Terradas, X., Tarrós, J., Buxo, R., Bosch, A., Chinchilla, J., Bogdanovich, I., Lopez, O. & Sana, M. 2015. Characterizing prehistoric archery: technical and functional analyses of the Neolithic Bows from La Draga (NE Iberian Peninsula). *Journal of Archaeological Science* 55, 166–173.

Podolefsky, A. 1984. Contemporary Warfare in the New Guinea Highlands. *Ethnology* 23, 73–87.

Polet, C, Dutour, O., Orban, R., Jadin, I. & Louryan, S. 1996. A Healed Wound Caused by a Flint Arrowhead in a Neolithic Human Innominate from the Trou Rosette (Furfooz, Belgium). *International Journal of Osteoarchaeology* 6, 414–420.

Potter, J.M. & Chuipka. 2010. Perimortem mutilation of human remains in an early village in the American Southwest: A case for ethnic violence. *Journal of Anthropological Archaeology* 29, 507–523.

Pritchard-Evans, E.E. 1960. Zande Cannibalism. *Journal of the Royal Anthropological Institute of Great Britain and Ireland* 90, 238–258.

Pryor, F. 1976. A neolithic mutiple burial from Fengate, Peterborough. *Antiquity* 50, 232–233.

Pyke, G. & Yiouni. 1996. *Nea Nikomedia 1: The Excavation of an Early Neolithic Village in Northern Greece 1961–1964 (edited by Wardle, K.A.)*. London, The British School at Athens.

Redfern, R.C. 2009. Does Cranial Trauma Provide Evidence for Projectile Weaponry in Late Iron Age Dorset? *Oxford Journal of Archaeology* 28, 399–424.

Richter, D.K. 1983. The Iroquois Experience. *William and Mary Quarterly* 40, 528–559.

Robb, J. 2009. People of Stone: Stelae, Personhood, and Society in Prehistoric Europe. *Journal of Archaeological Method and Theory* 16, 162–183.

Robb, J., Elster, E.S., Isetti, E., Knüsel, C.J., Tafuri, M.A. & Traverso, A. 2015. Cleaning the dead: Neolithic ritual processing of human bone at Scaloria Cave, Italy. *Antiquity* 89, 39–54.

Rodnick, D. 1939. An Assibone Horse-Raiding Expedition. *American Anthropologist* 41, 611–616.

Roksandic, M., Djuric, M., Rakočevic, Seguin, K. 2006 Interpersonal Violence at Lepenski Vir Mesolithic/Neolithic Complex of the Iron Gates Gorge (Serbia-Romania). *American Journal of Physical Anthropology* 129, 339–348.

Rowlands, M.J. 2004. Defence: a factor in the organization of settlements. In Ucko, P.J., Tringham, R. & Dimbleby, G.W. (eds), *Man, settlement and urbanism*, 447–462. London, Duckworth.

Rowley-Conwy, P. 2004. How the West Was Lost. A Reconsideration of Agricultural Origins in Britain, Ireland and Southern Scandinavia. *Current Anthropology* 45, 83–113.

Rubinetto, V., Appolonia L., De Leo, S., Serra, M. & Borghi, A. 2014. A Petrographic Study of the Anthropomorphic Stelae from the Megalithic Area of Saint-Martin-de-Corléans (Aosta, Northern Italy). *Archaeometry* 56, 927–950.

Runnels C.N., Payne, C., Rifkind, N.V., White, C. & Wolff, N.P. 2009. Warfare in Neolithic Thessaly. *Hesperia* 78, 165–194.

Sakaguchi, T., Morin, J. & Dickie, R. 2010. Defensibility of large prehistoric sites in the Mid-Fraser region on the Canadian Plateau. *Journal of Archaeological Science* 37, 1171–1185.

Sarauw, T. 2007. Male symbols or warrior identities? The 'archery burials' of the Danish Bell Beaker Culture. *Journal of Anthropological Archaeology* 26, 65–87.

Scarre, C (ed.) 1984. *Ancient France: Neolithic Societies and Their Landscapes*. Edinburgh, Edinburgh Univeristy Press.

Scarre, C. 1998. Arenas of Action? Enclosure Entrances in Neolithic Western France c. 3500–2500 BC. *Proceedings of the Prehistoric Society* 64, 115–117.

Scarre, C. (ed.) 2013. *The Human Past*. London, Thames & Hudson.

Schulting, R. 2012. Skeletal evidence for interpersonal violence: beyond mortuary monuments in southern Britain. In Schulting, R. & Fibiger, L (eds), in *Sticks, Stones, and Broken Bones: Neolithic Violence in a European Perspective*, 223–249. Oxford, Oxford University Press.

Schulting, R. 2013. War Without Warriors: The Nature of Interpersonal Conflict before the Emergence of Formalized Warrior Elites. In Ralph, S. (ed.), *The Archaeology of Violence: Interdisciplinary Approaches*, 19–36. New York, Suny Press.

Schulting, R.J. & Wysocki, M. 2005. "In this chambered tumulus were found cleft skulls": an assessment of the evidence for cranial trauma in the British Neolithic. *Proceedings of the Prehistoric Society* 71, 107–138.

Schumacher, T.X. 2002. Some Remarks on the Origin and Chronology of Halberds in Europe. *Oxford Journal of Archaeology* 21, 263–288.

Schutkowski, H., Schultz, M. & Holzgraefe, M. 1996. Fatal Wounds in a Late Neolithic Double Inhumation – A Probable Case of Meningitis Following Trauma. *International Journal of Osteoarchaeology* 6, 179–184.

Seeman, M.F. 1988. Ohio Hopewell Trophy-Skull Artifacts as Evidence for Competition in Middle Woodland Societies. *American Antiquity* 53, 565–577.

Sharples, N. 1991. *Maiden Castle: Excvations and Field Survey* 1985–6. London, English Heritage.

Shelach, G., Raphael, K. & Jaffe, Y. 2011. Sanzuodian: the structure, function and social significance of the earliest stone fortified sites in China. *Antiquity* 85, 11–26.

Sherrat, A. 1997. The Transformation of Early Agrarian Europe: The Later Neolithic and Copper Age 4500–2500 BC. In Cunliffe, B. (ed.), *Prehistoric Europe: An Illustrated History*, 167–201. Oxford, Oxford University Press.

Sillitoe, P. 1977. Land Shortage and War in New Guinea. *Ethnology* 16, 71–81.

Silva, A.M. & Marques, R. 2010. An arrowhead injury in a Neolithic human axis from the natural cave of Lapa do Bugio (Sesimbra, Portugal). *Anthropological Science* 118, 185–189.

Silva, A.M., Boaventura, R., Ferreira, M.T., Marques, R. 2013. Skeletal evidence of interpersonal violence from Portuguese Late Neolithic collective burials: an overview. In Schulting, R. & Fibiger, L (eds), in *Sticks, Stones, and Broken Bones: Neolithic Violence in a European Perspective*, 317–341. Oxford, Oxford University Press.

Skeates, J. 2000. The Social Dynamics of Enclosure in the Neolithic of the Tavoliere, South-East Italy. *Journal of Mediterranean Archaeology* 13, 155–188.

Smith, M. 2009. Bloody Stone Age. *Current Archaeology* 230, 12–19.

Smith, M. & Brickley, M. 2007. Boles Barrow: Witness to Ancient Violence. *British Archaeology* 93, 22–28.

Smith, M.J., Brickley, M.B. & Leach, S.L. 2007. Experimental evidence for lithic projectile injuries: improving indentification of an under-recognised phenomenon. *Journal of Archaeological Science* 34, 540–533.

Soriano, I., Gibaja, J.F., Vila, L. 2015. Open Warfare or the Odd Skirmish? Bell Beaker Violence in the North-Eastern Iberian Peninsula. *Oxford Journal of Archaeology* 34, 157–183.

Soudský, B. 1962. The Neolithic Site of Bylany. *Antiquity* XXXVI, 190–200.

Souvatzi, S. and Skafida, E. 2003. Neolithic Communties and Symbolic Meaning (Perceptions and Expressions of Symbolic and Social Structures at Late Neolithic Dimini, Thessaly). In Nikolova, L (ed.), *Early Symbolic Systems for Communication in Southeast Europe* (Vol. 2), 429–442. Oxford, Archaeopress, BAR International Series 1139.

Speilmann, A. & Eder, J.F. 1994. Hunters and Farmers: Then and Now. *Annual Review of Anthropology* 23, 303–323.

Standen, V.G. and Arriaza, B.T. 2000. Trauma in the Preceramic Coastal Populations of Northern Chile: Violence or Occupational Hazard? *American Journal of Physical Anthropology* 112, 239–249.

Standen, V.S. & Arriaza, B.T. 2000. Trauma in the Preceramic Coastal Populations of Northern Chile: Violence or Occupational Hazards? *American Journal of Physical Anthropology* 112, 239 249.

Sterud, E., R.K. Evans and J.A. Rasson. 1984. Ex Balcanis Lux? Recent Developments in Neolithic and Chalcolithic Southeast Europe. *American Antiquity* 49, 713–741.

Stevanovic, J. 1997. The Age of Clay: The Social Dynamics of House Destruction. *Journal of Anthropological Archaeology* 16, 334–395.

Storey, R. 2014. Classic Maya warfare and skeletal trophies: victims and aggressors. In Martin, D.L. & Anderson, C.P. (eds), *Biological and Forensic Perspectives on Violence*, 120–133. Cambridge, Cambridge University Press.

Talalay, L.E. 2004. Heady Business: Skulls, Heads, and Decapitation in Neolithic Anatolia and Greece. *Journal of Mediterranean Archaeology* 17, 139–163.

Teschler-Nicola, M. 2013. The Early Neolithic site Asparn/Schletz (Lower Austria): anthropological evidence of interpersonal violence. In R. Schulting & L. Fibiger (eds), *Sticks, Stones and Broken Bones: Neolithic Violence in a European Perspective*, 101–120. Oxford, Oxford University Press.

Teschler-Nicola, M, Gerold, F., Bujatti-Narbeshuber, M., Prohaska, T., Latkoczy, Ch., Stingeder, G. & Watkins, M. 1999. Evidence of Genocide 7000 BP – Neolithic Paradigm and Geo-Climatic Reality. *Collegium Antropologicum* 23, 437–450.

Thorpe, I.J.N. 2003. Anthropology, Archaeology, and the Origin of Warfare. *World Archaeology* 35, 145–165.

Thorpe, N. 2006. Fighting and Feuding in Neolithic and Bronze Age Britain and Ireland. In Otto, T., Thrane, H. & Vankilde, H. (eds), *Warfare and Society: Archaeological and Anthroplogical Perspectives*, 141–166. Aarhus, Aarhus University Press.

Towrie, S. 2011. Tomb of the Eagles Remains Paint a Darker Picture of Neolithic Orkney. http://www.orkneyjar.com/archaeology/2011/03/16/tomb-of-the-eagles-remains-paint-a-darker-picture-of-neolithic-orkney/.

Tringham, R. 1972. Territorial demarcation of prehisitoric settlements. In Ucko, P.J., Tringham, R. Dimbleby, G.W. (eds), Man, settlement and urbanism, 463–476. London, Duckworth.

Trautmann, A.E. & Fenton, T.W. 2005. A Case of Historic Cannibalism in the American West: Implications for Southwestern Archaeology. *American Antiquity* 70, 321–341.

Trubitt, M-B, D. 2003. The Production and Exchange of Marine Shell Prestige Goods. *Journal of Archaeological Research* 11, 243–277.

Tung, T.A. 2008. Dismembering bodies for Display: A Bioarchaeological Study of Trophy Heads from the Wari site of Concho pata, Peru. *American Journal of Physical Anthropology* 136, 294–308.

Turek, J. 2015. Bell Beaker stone wrist-guards as symbolic male orna-ment. The significance of ceremonial warfare in 3rd millennium BC central Europe. In M. P. Prieto Martínez & L. Salanova (eds), *The Bell Beaker Transition in Europe: Mobility and Local Evolution During the 3rd Millennium BC*, 28–40. Oxford & Philadelphia, Oxbow.

Turner II, C.G. & Morris, N. T. 1970. A Massacre at Hopi. *American Antiquity* 35, 320–331.

Van Andel, T.H. & Runnels, C.N. 1995. The earliest farmers in Europe. *Antiquity* 69, 481–500.

Van Derwarker, A. and Wilson, G. 2016. War, Food, and Structural Violence in the Mississipian Central Illinois Valley. In VanDerwarker, A. & Wilson, G,D. *The Archaeology of Food and Warfare*, 75–105. doi: 10.1007/978–3–319–18506–4_5, © Springer, Switzerland.

Vankilde, H. 2003. Commerative Tales: Archaeological Responses to Modern Myth, Politics and War. *World Archaeology* 35, 126–144.

Vankilde, H. 2003. Commemorative tales: archaeological responses to mod-ern myth, politics *and* war. *World Archaeology* 35, 126–144.

Vankilde, H. 2006. Archaeology and War: Presentations of Warriors and Peasants in Archaeological Interpretations. In Otto, T., Thrane, H. & Vankilde, H. *Warfare and Society: Archaeological and Anthroplogical Perspectives*, 57–74. Aarhus, Aarhus University Press.

Vankilde, H. Warriors and Warrior Institutions in Copper Age Europe. In Otto, T., Thrane, H. & and Vankilde, H., *Warfare and Society: Archaeological and Anthroplogical Perspectives*, 393–422. Aarhus, Aarhus University Press (2006).

Vankilde, H. 2015. Conflict and War, Archaeology of: Weapons and Artifacts'.In Wright, J.D. (ed.), *International Encyclopedia of the Social & Behavioral Sciences*, 607–613. Oxford, Elsevier.

Vazetti, A., Vidale, M., Gallinaro, M., Frayer, D.W. & Bondioli, L. 2010. The Iceman as a burial. *Antiquity* 84, 681–692.

Vegas, J.I., Armendariz, A., Exteberria, F, Fernandez, M.S. & Herrasti, L. 2012. Prehistoric Violence in northern Spain: San Juan ante Portam Latinam. In Schulting, R.J. & Fibiger, L (eds), *Sticks, Stones and Broken Bones: Skeletal Evidence for Interpersonal Violence in Europe*, 265–302. Oxford, Oxford University Press.

Veniamov, I. 1984. *Notes of the Islands of the Unalashka District* (trans. By Black T. & Geoghegan, R.H., ed. Pierce, R.A.). Fairbanks/Ontario, University of Alaska/Limestone Press.

Vencl. S. 1984. War and Warfare in Archaeology. *Journal of Anthropological Archaeology* 3, 116–132.

Vencl, S. 2009, Stone Age Warfare. In Carman, J. & Harding, A. (eds), *Ancient Warfare: Archaeological Perspectives*, 57–72. Stroud, The History Press.

Vilaça, A. 2000. Relations between Funerary Cannibalism and Warfare Cannibalism: The Question of Predation. *Ethnos* 65, 83–106.

Villa, P. 1992. Cannibalism in Prehistoric Europe. *Evolutionary Anthropology* 1, 93–104.

Villa, P., Bouville, C., Courtin, J., Helmer, D., Mahieu, E., Shipman, P. & Belluomini, G. 1986. Cannibalism in the Neolithic. *Science* 233, 431–437.

Villa, P. & Courtin, J. 1991. Cannibalism in the Neolithic. *Nature* 351, 613–614.

Von Lettow-Vorbeck, C.L. & Pastor Abascal, I. 2003. The Ciempozuelos Necropolis Skull: a Case of Double Trepanation? *International Journal of Osteoarchaeology* 13, 213–221.

Wahl, J. Trautmann, I. 2013. The Neolithic Massacre at Talheim: a pivotal find in conflict archaeology. In Schulting, R. & Fibiger, L. (eds), in *Sticks, Stones, and Broken Bones: Neolithic Violence in a European Perspective*, 77–100. Oxford, Oxford University Press.

Walker, P.L. 1989. Cranial Injuries As Evidence of Violence in Prehistoric Southern California. *American Journal of Physical Anthropology* 80, 313–323.

Walker, P. L. 2001. A Bioarchaeological Perspective on the History of Violence. *Annual Review of Anthropology* 30, 573–596.

Wallis, R.J. 2014. Re-examining stone 'wrist-guards' as evidence for falconry in later prehistoric Britain. *Antiquity* 88, 411–424.

Wardle, K.A. (ed.) 1996. *Nea Nikomedia 1: The Excavation of an Early Neolithic Village in Northern Greece 1961–1964*. London, The British School at Athens.

Westermann, J. 2007. Stepping from the Male to the Warrior Identity: Male Identity in Late Neolithic/Early Bronze Age Europe, 2800–2300 BC. In Bliujienė, A. (ed), *Weapons, Weaponry and Man: In Memorian Vytautas Kazakevičius*, 22–31. Klaipėda, Klaipėda University Press.

Wheeler, R.E.M. 1943. *Maiden Castle, Dorset*. Oxford, Reports of the Research Committee of the Society of Antiquaries.

Whittle, A. 1996. *Europe in the Neolithic: the creation of new worlds*. Cambridge, Cambridge University Press.

Whittle, A, Bayliss, A. & Wysocki, M. 2007. Once in a Lifetime: the Date of the Wayland's Smithy Long Barrow. *Cambridge Archaeological Journal* 17 (Supplement S1), 103–121.

Whittle, A., Healy, F. & Bayliss, A. 2011. Gathering Time: Dating the Early Neolithic Enclosures of Southern Britain and Ireland (Vols 1 & 2). Oxford, Oxbow.

Wild, E.M., Stadler, P., Häußer, A., Kutschera, W., Steier, P., Teschler-Nicola, M., Wahl, J. & Windl, H.J. 2004. Neolithic Massacres: Local Skirmishes or General Warfare in Europe? *Radiocarbon* 46, 377–385.

Wilson, T. 1901. Arrow Wounds. *American Anthropologist* 3, 513–531.

Wolfe Steadman, D. 2008. Warfare Related Trauma at Orendorf, A Middle Mississipian Site in West-Central Illinois. *American Journal of Physical Anthropology* 136, 51–64.

Woodward, A., Hunter, J., Ixer, R., Roe, F., Potts, P.J., Webb, P.C., Watson, J.S. & Jones, M.C. 2006. Beaker age bracers in England: sources, function and use. *Antiquity* 80, 530–543.

Worrall. S. 2014. Amazon Warriors Did Indeed Fight and Die Like Men. news.nationalgeographic.com/news/2014/10/141029-amazons-scythians-hunger-games-herodotus-ice-princess-tatoo-cannabis/.

Wysocki, M. & Whittle, A. 2000. Diversity, lifestyles and rites: new biological and archaeological evidence from British Earlier Neolithic mortuary assemblages. *Antiquity* 285, 591–601.

Zäuner, S.P., J. Wahl, Y. Boyadziev and I. Aslanis. 2013. A 6000 Year-Old Hand Amputation from Bulgaria The Oldest Case from South-East Europe. *International Journal of Osteoarchaeology* 23, 618–625.

Zefferman, M.R. & Mathew, S. 2015. An Evolutionary Theory of Large-Scale Human Warfare: Group-Structured Cultural Selection. *Evolutionary Anthropology* 24, 50–61.

Zimmerman, L.J. & Bradley, L.E. 1993. The Crow Creek Massacre: Initial Coalescent Warfare and Speculations About the Genesis of Exctended Coalescent. *Plains Anthropologist 38, Memoir 27*, 215–226.

Žukauskaitė, J. 2009. Images of the Horse and Horseman in Corded Ware Culture Studies. Archaeologia Baltica 11, 32–36.

Index